At Sylvan, we believe that everyone can master math skills, and we are glad you have chosen our resources to help your children experience the joy of mathematics as they build crucial reasoning skills. We know that time spent reinforcing lessons learned in school will contribute to understanding and mastery.

Success in math requires more than just memorizing basic facts and algorithms; it also requires children to make connections between the real world and math concepts in order to solve problems. Successful problem solvers will be ready for the challenges of mathematics as they advance to more complex topics and encounter new problems both in school and at home.

We use a research-based, step-by-step process in teaching math at Sylvan that includes thought-provoking math problems and activities. As students increase their success as problem solvers, they become more confident. With increasing confidence, students build even more success. The design of the Sylvan workbooks lays out a roadmap for mathematical learning that is designed to lead your child to success in school.

We're excited to partner with you to support the development of confident, successful, and independent learners!

The Sylvan Team

4th Grade
Jumbo Math Success
Workbook

Published in the United States by Random House, Inc., New York, and in Canada by Random House of Canada Limited, Toronto.

This book was previously published with the title *4th Grade Super Math Success* as a trade paperback by Sylvan Learning, Inc., an imprint of Penguin Random House LLC, in 2010.

www.sylvanlearning.com

Created by Smarterville Productions LLC
Producer & Editorial Direction: The Linguistic Edge
Producer: TJ Trochlil McGreevy
Writer: Amy Kraft
Cover and Interior Illustrations: Shawn Finley, Tim Goldman, and Duendes del Sur
Cover Design: Suzanne Lee
Layout and Art Direction: SunDried Penguin
Director of Product Development: Russell Ginns

First Edition

ISBN: 978-0-307-47920-4

This book is available at special discounts for bulk purchases for sales promotions or premiums. For more information, write to Special Markets/Premium Sales, 1745 Broadway, MD 6-2, New York, New York 10019 or e-mail specialmarkets@randomhouse.com.

PRINTED IN CHINA

Basic Math Success Contents

Math Games & Puzzles Contents

Math in the Environment

Math in Action Contents

Graphs & Data

4th Grade
Basic Math Success

Number Words

WRITE the number words for each number.

HINT: Commas make big numbers easier to read. A comma belongs after the millions place and after the thousands place in both the number and its written form.

Example:

3,694,527	
3,000,000	three million
600,000	six hundred thousand
90,000	ninety thousand
4,000	four thousand
500	five hundred
20	twenty
7	seven

3,694,527 in written form is three million, six hundred ninety-four thousand, five hundred twenty-seven.

1. **2,439**   two thousand, four hundred thirty-nine

2. **41,582**

3. **736,120**

4. **5,824,416**

5. **9,301,558**

What's My Number?

WRITE the number.

HINT: Don't forget the comma after the millions place and the thousands place. Starting at the right, count every three digits to the left and add a comma.

1. __6,942__   six thousand, nine hundred forty-two

2. _____   five hundred sixty-four thousand, one hundred eighty-one

3. _____   two million, two hundred twenty-three thousand,
                        eight hundred forty-six

4. _____   ninety thousand, three hundred thirty-seven

5. _____   four million, one hundred nineteen thousand,
                        six hundred seventy-three

6. _____   seven thousand, three hundred fourteen

7. _____   one million, eight hundred eighty-two thousand,
                        four hundred fifty

8. _____   seventy-six thousand, five hundred eight

9. _____   two hundred thirty thousand, seven hundred twenty-nine

10. _____   seven million, four hundred ninety-one thousand,
                        two hundred seventy-seven

Find Your Place

IDENTIFY the place of each digit. Then WRITE the digit.

Example:

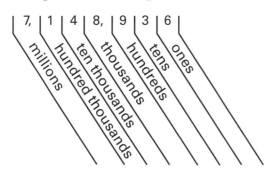

1. **8,523,762**

8	millions
5	hundred thousands
2	ten thousands
3	thousands
7	hundreds
6	tens
2	ones

2. **1,994,857**

___	millions
___	hundred thousands
___	ten thousands
___	thousands
___	hundreds
___	tens
___	ones

3. **4,370,284**

___	millions
___	hundred thousands
___	ten thousands
___	thousands
___	hundreds
___	tens
___	ones

4. **6,251,319**

___	millions
___	hundred thousands
___	ten thousands
___	thousands
___	hundreds
___	tens
___	ones

5. **7,842,523**

___	millions
___	hundred thousands
___	ten thousands
___	thousands
___	hundreds
___	tens
___	ones

6. **5,719,688**

___	millions
___	hundred thousands
___	ten thousands
___	thousands
___	hundreds
___	tens
___	ones

High Fives

FIND the 5 in each number. WRITE the place of each 5.

1. 3,533,972   _____ hundred thousands _____ place

2. 6,085,427   _____ place

3. 5,174,819   _____ place

4. 2,940,758   _____ place

5. 8,258,133   _____ place

6. 1,719,605   _____ place

7. 3,562,394   _____ place

8. 9,894,541   _____ place

Mismatched

WRITE > or < in each box.

907 > 738   612 ☐ 599
1   2

776 ☐ 862   423 ☐ 2,423
3   4

5,275 ☐ 891   1,006 ☐ 950
5   6

6,472 ☐ 3,565   8,717 ☐ 7,818
7   8

4,063 ☐ 4,157   9,899 ☐ 10,099
9   10

32,751 ☐ 51,336   12,655 ☐ 12,461
11   12

103,003 > 88,724   642,195 ☐ 448,449
13   14

854,545 ☐ 548,484   365,272 ☐ 365,709
15   16

Matched or Mismatched?

WRITE >, <, or = in each box.

4,080,867 ☐ 6,959,864   2,777,549 ☐ 1,696,093
        1   2

5,623,452 ☐ 5,623,452   2,785,975 ☐ 1,536,698
        3   4

7,928,059 ☐ 9,507,088   6,471,341 ☐ 8,459,450
        5   6

4,892,580 ☐ 4,892,580   3,470,189 ☐ 3,578,206
        7   8

1,116,896 ☐ 1,128,553   8,295,416 ☐ 8,290,643
        9   10

7,580,088 ☐ 7,583,130   5,494,364 ☐ 5,492,964
       11   12

9,746,931 ☐ 9,746,959   6,016,551 ☐ 6,016,551
       13   14

2,173,219 ☐ 2,173,419   4,999,016 ☐ 4,999,009
       15   16

Which One?

CIRCLE the largest number in each row.

5,036	6,874	5,239	6,790
2. 10,175	9,628	11,160	10,181
26,696	25,217	28,879	27,688
4. 680,391	634,805	650,864	678,945
3,085,780	3,162,983	3,112,536	3,186,797
6. 7,194,027	7,198,003	7,006,472	7,156,321

Which One?

CIRCLE the smallest number in each row.

1. 3,420   4,038   3,877   3,975

2. 16,516   14,359   15,078   14,238

3. 45,348   46,070   45,297   45,904

4. 912,531   852,268   902,277   885,648

5. 4,163,588   4,647,766   4,531,690   4,290,312

6. 6,267,832   6,299,421   6,267,828   6,301,005

3

Round About

Rounding makes numbers easier to work with.

Numbers that end in 1 through 499 get rounded **down** to the nearest thousand.

Numbers that end in 500 through 999 get rounded **up** to the nearest thousand.

Numbers that end in 1 through 4,999 get rounded **down** to the nearest ten thousand.

Numbers that end in 5,000 through 9,999 get rounded **up** to the nearest ten thousand.

ROUND to the nearest thousand.

1. 1,024 _____

2. 7,885 _____

3. 6,133 _____

4. 8,647 _____

5. 2,712 _____

6. 4,603 _____

7. 9,428 _____

8. 4,530 _____

9. 5,499 _____

ROUND to the nearest ten thousand.

10. 83,723 _____

11. 17,607 _____

12. 23,652 _____

13. 58,149 _____

14. 62,996 _____

15. 74,342 _____

16. 15,890 _____

17. 44,444 _____

18. 33,501 _____

Round About

Numbers that end in 1 through 49,999 get rounded **down** to the nearest hundred thousand.

635,612 ⟶ 600,000

Numbers that end in 50,000 through 99,999 get rounded **up** to the nearest hundred thousand.

659,782 ⟶ 700,000

Numbers that end in 1 through 499,999 get rounded **down** to the nearest million.

1,422,034 ⟶ 1,000,000

Numbers that end in 500,000 through 999,999 get rounded **up** to the nearest million.

1,599,278 ⟶ 2,000,000

ROUND to the nearest hundred thousand.

1. 707,269 _____

2. 595,389 _____

3. 133,805 _____

4. 360,056 _____

5. 225,173 _____

6. 968,615 _____

7. 448,883 _____

8. 556,724 _____

ROUND to the nearest million.

9. 3,248,955 _____

10. 9,313,548 _____

11. 4,701,205 _____

12. 7,119,125 _____

13. 5,212,111 _____

14. 1,492,166 _____

15. 2,566,089 _____

16. 6,430,209 _____

Guess and Check

Estimating is making a reasonable guess about something. How many jellybeans are on this page? WRITE your estimate. Then CIRCLE a group of 20 jellybeans. WRITE a new estimate. CHECK page 119 to see how close your estimates were.

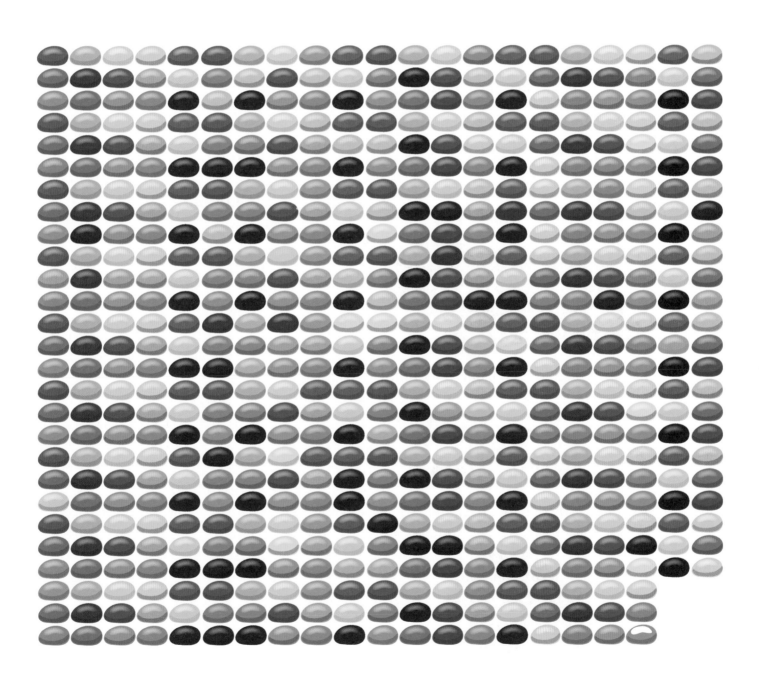

Estimate 1: _____   Estimate 2: _____   Check: _____

Match Up

DRAW a line to match each picture with a reasonable estimate.

Pages in a dictionary

50

Staples in a box

3,000,000

Stars visible on a clear, dark night

1,800

Cookies in a package

200,000

Leaves on a tree

5,000

It All Adds Up

To add large numbers, start with the ones and work left.

5 3,0 4 5 + 1 2,2 3 0 = 5	5 3,0 4 5 + 1 2,2 3 0 = 7 5	5 3,0 4 5 + 1 2,2 3 0 = 2 7 5	5 3,0 4 5 + 1 2,2 3 0 = 5,2 7 5	5 3,0 4 5 + 1 2,2 3 0 = 6 5,2 7 5
Add the ones.	Add the tens.	Add the hundreds.	Add the thousands.	Add the ten thousands.

WRITE each sum.

1. 84,156
  + 3,812

2. 16,314
  + 1,142

3. 51,231
  + 2,724

4. 20,422
  + 9,262

5. 41,602
  + 17,113

6. 71,477
  + 23,120

7. 16,022
  + 10,171

8. 31,163
  + 48,101

9. 20,114
  + 20,122

10. 32,340
  + 52,413

11. 31,231
  + 34,411

12. 45,481
  + 14,214

Pick Apart

Partial sums is a method of addition, adding each place one at a time.

$$42,784$$
$$+\ 26,197$$

Add the numbers in the ten thousands place.	40,000 + 20,000 =	60,000
Add the numbers in the thousands place.	2,000 + 6,000 =	8,000
Add the numbers in the hundreds place.	700 + 100 =	800
Add the numbers in the tens place.	80 + 90 =	170
Add the numbers in the ones place.	4 + 7 = +	11
The answer is 60,000 + 8,000 + 800 + 170 + 11.		68,981

WRITE each sum using partial sums.

1. 52,228
   + 26,355

2. 31,496
   + 33,282

3. 71,024
   + 19,936

4. 47,343
   + 25,748

5. 11,433
   + 35,793

6. 48,733
   + 50,896

7. 12,114
   + 13,924

8. 53,742
   + 35,723

It All Adds Up

Whenever the sum is more than nine, carry the one over to the next place.

1 3 1,8 2 4 + 4 3,9 7 7 ‾‾‾‾‾‾‾‾‾‾‾ 1	1 1 3 1,8 2 4 + 4 3,9 7 7 ‾‾‾‾‾‾‾‾‾‾‾ 0 1	1 1 1 3 1,8 2 4 + 4 3,9 7 7 ‾‾‾‾‾‾‾‾‾‾‾ 8 0 1	1 1 1 3 1,8 2 4 + 4 3,9 7 7 ‾‾‾‾‾‾‾‾‾‾‾ 5,8 0 1	1 1 1 3 1,8 2 4 + 4 3,9 7 7 ‾‾‾‾‾‾‾‾‾‾‾ 7 5,8 0 1
Add the ones. 4 + 7 = 11	Add the tens. 1 + 2 + 7 = 10	Add the hundreds. 1 + 8 + 9 = 18	Add the thousands. 1 + 1 + 3 = 5	Add the ten thousands. 3 + 4 = 7

WRITE each sum.

1. 47,196
    + 2,986

2. 33,589
    + 7,820

3. 86,353
    + 5,975

4. 71,417
    + 4,826

5. 55,537
    + 13,484

6. 46,416
    + 51,624

7. 16,273
    + 16,876

8. 37,232
    + 18,099

9. 25,804
    + 52,209

10. 42,839
    + 46,399

11. 43,375
    + 19,707

12. 19,067
    + 23,755

Adding 5-Digit Numbers

It All Adds Up

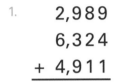

WRITE each sum.

1.
```
   2,989
   6,324
+  4,911
```

2.
```
   3,076
   8,144
+  3,885
```

3.
```
   7,623
   9,758
+  2,566
```

4.
```
   5,853
   4,610
+  7,899
```

5.
```
  35,118
   2,554
+  6,307
```

6.
```
  48,551
   1,964
+  5,213
```

7.
```
  12,457
  23,794
+ 29,381
```

8.
```
  36,680
  42,787
+ 16,632
```

9.
```
  19,237
   3,199
   8,513
+  3,551
```

10.
```
  25,864
  52,428
   7,445
+  1,197
```

11.
```
  48,319
  15,523
  22,993
+  4,701
```

12.
```
  10,832
  23,614
  11,513
+ 13,922
```

What's the Difference?

To subtract large numbers, start with the ones and work left.

7 4,6 6 7 − 2 3,0 5 3 4	7 4,6 6 7 − 2 3,0 5 3 1 4	7 4,6 6 7 − 2 3,0 5 3 6 1 4	7 4,6 6 7 − 2 3,0 5 3 1,6 1 4	7 4,6 6 7 − 2 3,0 5 3 5 1,6 1 4
Subtract the ones.	Subtract the tens.	Subtract the hundreds.	Subtract the thousands.	Subtract the ten thousands.

WRITE each difference.

1. 28,932
    − 7,211

2. 54,986
    − 1,950

3. 95,459
    − 2,026

4. 79,137
    − 2,035

5. 88,589
    − 75,460

6. 72,527
    − 21,314

7. 83,596
    − 22,191

8. 65,939
    − 22,415

9. 79,438
    − 74,110

10. 67,798
    − 45,058

11. 26,739
    − 12,114

12. 49,681
    − 10,330

What's the Difference?

Whenever the digit on top is smaller, regroup numbers from the next place to the left.

5 13 7 9,1 6̶ 3̶ – 1 7,4 5 9 ——— 4	5 13 7 9,1 6̶ 3̶ – 1 7,4 5 9 ——— 0 4	8 11 5 13 7 9,1̶ 6̶ 3̶ – 1 7,4 5 9 ——— 7 0 4	8 11 5 13 7 9̶,1̶ 6̶ 3̶ – 1 7,4 5 9 ——— 1,7 0 4	8 11 5 13 7 9̶,1̶ 6̶ 3̶ – 1 7,4 5 9 ——— 6 1,7 0 4
Subtract the ones. Regroup 1 from the tens place. $13 - 9 = 4$	Subtract the tens. $5 - 5 = 0$	Subtract the hundreds. Regroup 1 from the thousands place. $11 - 4 = 7$	Subtract the thousands. $8 - 7 = 1$	Subtract the ten thousands. $7 - 1 = 6$

WRITE each difference.

1. $\begin{array}{r} 50,635 \\ - 7,048 \\ \hline \end{array}$

2. $\begin{array}{r} 11,515 \\ - 3,648 \\ \hline \end{array}$

3. $\begin{array}{r} 66,723 \\ - 8,851 \\ \hline \end{array}$

4. $\begin{array}{r} 78,596 \\ - 8,987 \\ \hline \end{array}$

5. $\begin{array}{r} 46,932 \\ - 21,374 \\ \hline \end{array}$

6. $\begin{array}{r} 59,652 \\ - 10,867 \\ \hline \end{array}$

7. $\begin{array}{r} 92,821 \\ - 86,474 \\ \hline \end{array}$

8. $\begin{array}{r} 82,714 \\ - 33,263 \\ \hline \end{array}$

9. $\begin{array}{r} 91,894 \\ - 16,759 \\ \hline \end{array}$

10. $\begin{array}{r} 33,862 \\ - 19,079 \\ \hline \end{array}$

11. $\begin{array}{r} 54,692 \\ - 24,715 \\ \hline \end{array}$

12. $\begin{array}{r} 36,002 \\ - 12,820 \\ \hline \end{array}$

Trade First

With the **trade-first** method, you do all of the regrouping at once.

6 7,6 3 4 − 2 1,9 2 8	^{6 16 2 14} 6 7̶,6̶ 3̶ 4̶ − 2 1,9 2 8	^{6 16 2 14} 6 7̶,6̶ 3̶ 4̶ − 2 1,9 2 8 4 5,7 0 6
Look for any place where the bottom digit is too large to be subtracted from the top digit.	Do all of the regrouping at once.	Then subtract each place.

WRITE each difference using the trade-first method.

1.   46,256
    − 8,931

2.   74,597
    − 9,068

3.   31,042
    − 2,305

4.   50,510
    − 6,954

5.   24,414
    − 19,599

6.   91,412
    − 33,649

7.   66,135
    − 40,697

8.   22,792
    − 10,856

9.   99,087
    − 13,459

10.   49,516
     − 21,686

11.   77,188
     − 37,519

12.   40,770
     − 27,158

Subtracting 5-Digit Numbers

What's the Difference

WRITE each difference.

HINT: Try using the methods of the last two pages, and decide which one works best for you.

1. 41,821 – 4,387	2. 64,253 – 1,746	3. 82,882 – 5,754	4. 96,630 – 7,316
5. 91,705 – 3,028	6. 19,052 – 1,416	7. 24,008 – 9,725	8. 56,041 – 4,550
9. 70,151 – 44,302	10. 53,314 – 20,728	11. 28,526 – 16,549	12. 38,607 – 36,594
13. 65,087 – 24,719	14. 79,662 – 48,845	15. 17,391 – 14,999	16. 81,139 – 73,252

Number Drop-off

Front-end estimation is a fast way to determine approximately how large a sum or difference will be. For front-end estimation, make all but the leftmost digit of each number zero.

$$
\begin{array}{r}
8\,1,2\,0\,7 \\
+\ \ 6,5\,5\,2 \\
\end{array}
\longrightarrow
\begin{array}{r}
8\,0,0\,0\,0 \\
+\ \ 6,0\,0\,0 \\
\hline
8\,6,0\,0\,0 \\
\end{array}
$$

81,207 becomes 80,000.
6,552 becomes 6,000.
80,000 + 6,000 = 86,000
81,207 + 6,552 = 87,759

ESTIMATE each sum or difference using front-end estimation. Then WRITE the actual sum or difference to see how close your estimate was.

1.
$$
\begin{array}{r}
8,576 \\
+\ 1,259 \\
\end{array}
\qquad + \underline{\hspace{3cm}}
$$

2.
$$
\begin{array}{r}
9,662 \\
-\ 2,314 \\
\end{array}
\qquad - \underline{\hspace{3cm}}
$$

3.
$$
\begin{array}{r}
30,862 \\
+\ 2,775 \\
\end{array}
\qquad + \underline{\hspace{3cm}}
$$

4.
$$
\begin{array}{r}
46,237 \\
-\ 4,669 \\
\end{array}
\qquad - \underline{\hspace{3cm}}
$$

5.
$$
\begin{array}{r}
40,927 \\
+\ 35,290 \\
\end{array}
\qquad + \underline{\hspace{3cm}}
$$

6.
$$
\begin{array}{r}
99,730 \\
-\ 57,594 \\
\end{array}
\qquad - \underline{\hspace{3cm}}
$$

Rounding Estimates

Rounding numbers before adding and subtracting them often produces a closer estimate than using front-end estimation.

$$6\,8{,}2\,3\,1 \longrightarrow 7\,0{,}0\,0\,0$$
$$+1\,3{,}1\,7\,5 \longrightarrow +1\,0{,}0\,0\,0$$
$$8\,0{,}0\,0\,0$$

68,231 rounded to the nearest ten thousand is 70,000.

13,175 rounded to the nearest ten thousand is 10,000.

70,000 + 10,000 = 80,000

68,231 + 13,175 = 81,406

ESTIMATE each sum or difference by rounding to the nearest ten thousand. WRITE the actual sum or difference to see how close your estimate was.

1.
$$\begin{array}{r} 19{,}343 \\ +\ 40{,}489 \\ \hline \end{array}$$
+ _____

2.
$$\begin{array}{r} 53{,}677 \\ -\ 24{,}156 \\ \hline \end{array}$$
− _____

3.
$$\begin{array}{r} 65{,}563 \\ +\ 12{,}498 \\ \hline \end{array}$$
+ _____

4.
$$\begin{array}{r} 79{,}432 \\ -\ 42{,}722 \\ \hline \end{array}$$
− _____

5.
$$\begin{array}{r} 57{,}249 \\ +\ 28{,}501 \\ \hline \end{array}$$
+ _____

6.
$$\begin{array}{r} 64{,}205 \\ -\ 52{,}198 \\ \hline \end{array}$$
− _____

Pesky Products

A **multiplication table** shows the products you get when you multiply numbers in the first row with the numbers in the first column. WRITE the missing numbers on the multiplication table.

×	0	1	2	3	4	5	6	7	8	9	10
0	0	0	0	0	0		0	0		0	0
1		1	2		4	5		7	8		10
2	0		4	6		10	12		16	18	
3	0	3		9	12		18	21		27	30
4		4	8		16	20		28	32		40
5	0		10	15		25	30		40	45	
6	0	6		18	24		36	42		54	60
7		7	14		28	35		49	56		70
8	0		16	24		40	48		64	72	
9	0	9		27	36		54	63		81	90
10		10	20		40	50		70	80		100

Multiplication Facts

Computation Station

A **product** is the number you get when you multiply two numbers. WRITE each product.

1. 5 × 3 = _____   2. 8 × 9 = _____   3. 6 × 1 = _____   4. 2 × 7 = _____

5. 3 × 10 = _____   6. 6 × 6 = _____   7. 8 × 7 = _____   8. 5 × 0 = _____

9. 8 × 8 = _____   10. 5 × 2 = _____   11. 7 × 9 = _____   12. 10 × 10 = _____

13. 6   14. 1   15. 7   16. 9   17. 10   18. 5
   × 5   × 3   × 6   × 4   × 8   × 5

19. 9   20. 0   21. 5   22. 9   23. 6   24. 9
   × 3   × 1   × 2   × 9   × 4   × 2

25. 7   26. 10   27. 3   28. 7   29. 8   30. 4
   × 7   × 2   × 3   × 1   × 6   × 4

Picture It

When multiplying a two-digit number, think of it as tens and ones.

Example: 67 × 5 = ___335___

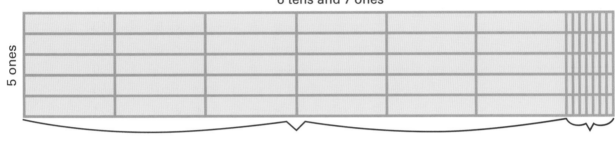

6 tens and 7 ones

5 ones

6 tens × 5 ones = 30 tens, or 300   7 ones × 5 ones = 35 ones, or 35

300 + 35 = 335   67 × 5 = 335

Use the pictures to help you answer the problems. WRITE each product.

1. **53 × 8** = _____

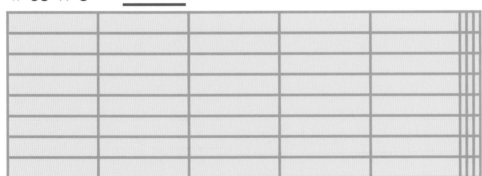

2. **39 × 4** = _____

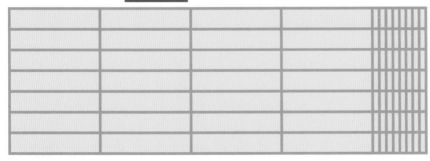

3. **48 × 7** = _____

Break It Down

Break down each problem into simple multiplication problems whose products can be added together. WRITE each product.

Example: 54 × 6 =   __324__

    54 = 10 + 10 + 10 + 10 + 10 + 4

10	×	6 =	60
10	×	6 =	60
10	×	6 =	60
10	×	6 =	60
10	×	6 =	60
4	×	6 =	+ 24
			324

1. 18 × 9 = _____

2. 46 × 5 = _____

3. 62 × 7 = _____

4. 57 × 3 = _____

5. 23 × 4 = _____

6. 35 × 8 = _____

8

Computation Station

WRITE each product.

Example:

72	72
× 4	× 4
8	288
Multiply the ones.	Multiply the tens.
2 × 4 = 8 ones	7 × 4 = 28 tens, or 280

1. 24
× 2

2. 79
× 1

3. 31
× 9

4. 44
× 2

5. 13
× 3

6. 62
× 4

7. 84
× 2

8. 93
× 2

9. 50
× 8

10. 64
× 2

11. 73
× 3

12. 20
× 7

13. 91
× 6

14. 63
× 2

15. 87
× 1

16. 40
× 9

17. 52
× 4

18. 71
× 5

Multidigit Multiplication

Computation Station

WRITE each product.

Example:

³65 × 7 ――― 5	³65 × 7 ――― 455
Multiply the ones. 5 × 7 = 35 ones Write 5 in the ones place and carry 3 tens.	Multiply the tens. 6 × 7 = 42 tens + 3 tens = 45 tens, or 450

1. 57 × 2

2. 96 × 3

3. 72 × 9

4. 35 × 6

5. 88 × 4

6. 43 × 7

7. 26 × 8

8. 65 × 5

9. 33 × 8

10. 16 × 3

11. 47 × 7

12. 74 × 4

13. 34 × 9

14. 76 × 8

15. 19 × 6

16. 53 × 4

17. 99 × 7

18. 85 × 9

Computation Station

WRITE each product.

Example:

⁵ 149 × 6 ‾‾4‾	²⁵ 149 × 6 ‾94‾	²⁵ 149 × 6 ‾894‾
Multiply the ones. 9 × 6 = 54 ones Write 4 in the ones place and carry 5 tens.	Multiply the tens. 4 × 6 = 24 tens + 5 tens = 29 tens, or 290 Write 9 in the tens place and carry 2 hundreds.	Multiply the hundreds. 1 × 6 = 6 hundreds + 2 hundreds = 8 hundreds, or 800.

1. 352
× 2

2. 438
× 4

3. 816
× 9

4. 142
× 6

5. 767
× 5

6. 295
× 7

7. 807
× 3

8. 182
× 5

9. 332
× 4

10. 675
× 1

11. 514
× 7

12. 270
× 9

13. 454
× 6

14. 563
× 2

15. 319
× 8

16. 272
× 5

17. 928
× 3

18. 198
× 9

Pick Apart

Partial products is a method of multiplication, multiplying each place one at a time.

	682
	× 7

Multiply the hundreds.   600 × 7 = 4,200
Multiply the tens.   80 × 7 =   560
Multiply the ones.   2 × 7 = + 14
Then add the numbers together.   4,774

WRITE each product using partial products.

1. 455
  ×   8

2. 372
  ×   2

3. 518
  ×   4

4. 796
  ×   5

5. 189
  ×   6

6. 231
  ×   8

7. 574
  ×   7

8. 387
  ×   3

9. 922
  ×   9

10. 437
  ×   5

Computation Station

When you multiply by a two-digit number, multiply one place at a time.

1 3 4 2 7 × 3 5 ‾‾‾‾‾ 2,1 3 5	2 4 2 7 × 3 5 ‾‾‾‾‾ 2,1 3 5 1 0	2 4 2 7 × 3 5 ‾‾‾‾‾ 2,1 3 5 8 1 0	2 4 2 7 × 3 5 ‾‾‾‾‾ 2,1 3 5 12,8 1 0	4 2 7 × 3 5 ‾‾‾‾‾ 2,1 3 5 + 1 2,8 1 0 ‾‾‾‾‾‾‾ 1 4,9 4 5
Multiply 427 by 5 ones.	Multiply 427 by 3 tens, starting with the ones place. 7 ones × 3 tens = 21 tens, or 210.	Next, multiply the tens place. 2 tens × 3 tens = 6 hundreds + 2 hundreds = 8 hundreds, or 800.	Next, multiply the hundreds place. 4 hundreds × 3 tens = 12 thousands.	Then add 2,135 and 12,810.

WRITE each product.

1. 54
× 21

2. 36
× 15

3. 63
× 45

4. 74
× 30

5. 49
× 72

6. 88
× 56

7. 90
× 47

8. 25
× 25

9. 77
× 13

10. 93
× 68

11. 41
× 19

12. 64
× 42

13. 7 3 1
× 12

14. 5 4 2
× 34

15. 8 4 0
× 65

16. 2 6 7
× 56

17. 3 9 5
× 27

18. 9 7 1
× 82

Pick Apart

Using partial products to multiply by a two-digit number works the same way as with a one-digit number.

Example:

							354
						×	62
Multiply the hundreds.	300	×	60	=			18,000
	300	×	2	=			600
Multiply the tens.	50	×	60	=			3,000
	50	×	2	=			100
Multiply the ones.	4	×	60	=			240
	4	×	2	=	+		8
Then add the numbers together.							21,948

WRITE each product using partial products.

1. 34
  × 26

2. 75
  × 42

3. 51
  × 37

4. 92
  × 48

5. 68
  × 16

6. 164
  × 35

7. 379
  × 11

8. 215
  × 59

9. 641
  × 76

10. 827
  × 63

Divide and Conquer

WRITE the missing numbers on each chart.

HINT: Divide the numbers in the top row by the number on the side.

÷	25	5	35	20	50	15	10	30	45	40
5	5									

÷	15	27	12	3	30	18	6	24	9	21
3										

÷	8	48	80	40	16	24	56	72	32	64
8										

÷	24	40	16	20	32	8	12	28	36	4
4										

÷	21	63	28	56	35	70	14	7	49	42
7										

÷	18	90	9	54	63	27	36	72	81	45
9										

Computation Station

A **quotient** is the number you get when you divide one number by another number.
WRITE each quotient.

1. $14 \div 7 =$ _____   2. $63 \div 9 =$ _____   3. $80 \div 8 =$ _____   4. $36 \div 4 =$ _____

5. $72 \div 8 =$ _____   6. $35 \div 5 =$ _____   7. $48 \div 6 =$ _____   8. $16 \div 2 =$ _____

9. $27 \div 3 =$ _____   10. $10 \div 10 =$ _____   11. $21 \div 7 =$ _____   12. $8 \div 1 =$ _____

13. $5 \overline{)45}$ 14. $9 \overline{)90}$ 15. $6 \overline{)30}$ 16. $9 \overline{)81}$ 17. $3 \overline{)15}$

18. $6 \overline{)12}$ 19. $7 \overline{)49}$ 20. $10 \overline{)100}$ 21. $8 \overline{)64}$ 22. $5 \overline{)20}$

23. $7 \overline{)7}$ 24. $9 \overline{)27}$ 25. $3 \overline{)12}$ 26. $7 \overline{)70}$ 27. $4 \overline{)16}$

28. $9 \overline{)45}$ 29. $1 \overline{)5}$ 30. $4 \overline{)32}$ 31. $9 \overline{)72}$ 32. $7 \overline{)63}$

Picture It

Use the pictures to help you find the quotients. WRITE each quotient.

HINT: Imagine you are sharing the shaded blocks with the number of people in the divisor (the number being used to divide).

5 rows of 12

Example: 60 ÷ 5 = __12__

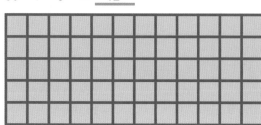
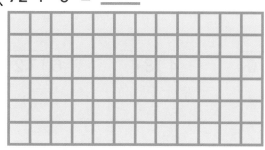

1. 88 ÷ 8 = _____

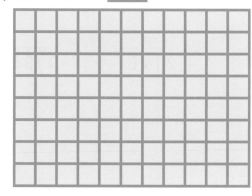

2. 72 ÷ 6 = _____

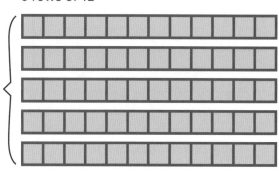

3. 32 ÷ 2 = _____

4. 44 ÷ 11 = _____

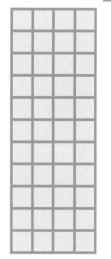

5. 56 ÷ 4 = _____

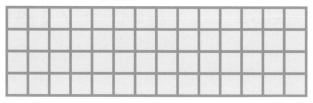

Computation Station

DIVIDE two-digit numbers.

Example:

$4\overline{)96}$	$\begin{array}{r} 2 \\ 4\overline{)96} \\ 8 \end{array}$	$\begin{array}{r} 2 \\ 4\overline{)96} \\ -8 \\ \hline 1 \end{array}$	$\begin{array}{r} 2 \\ 4\overline{)96} \\ -8 \\ \hline 16 \end{array}$	$\begin{array}{r} 24 \\ 4\overline{)96} \\ -8 \\ \hline 16 \\ -16 \\ \hline 0 \end{array}$
Start by looking at the first number of the dividend (the number that's being divided). Think of a multiple of 4 that is near 9 but not greater than 9.	$4 \times 2 = 8$ Write 2 above the 9 and 8 below it.	Subtract 8 from 9.	Bring the 6 down next to the 1. Now find $16 \div 4$.	$4 \times 4 = 16$ Write 4 in the ones place.

WRITE each quotient.

1. $5\overline{)90}$
2. $4\overline{)84}$
3. $6\overline{)72}$
4. $3\overline{)63}$
5. $2\overline{)48}$
6. $9\overline{)99}$

7. $7\overline{)91}$
8. $2\overline{)92}$
9. $5\overline{)85}$
10. $3\overline{)96}$
11. $2\overline{)50}$
12. $3\overline{)81}$

13. $2\overline{)68}$
14. $6\overline{)78}$
15. $8\overline{)96}$
16. $5\overline{)55}$
17. $7\overline{)84}$
18. $2\overline{)98}$

Computation Station

DIVIDE three-digit numbers.

Example:

$6\overline{)354}$	$\begin{array}{r}5\\6\overline{)354}\\30\end{array}$	$\begin{array}{r}5\\6\overline{)354}\\-30\\\hline 5\end{array}$	$\begin{array}{r}5\\6\overline{)354}\\-30\\\hline 54\end{array}$	$\begin{array}{r}59\\6\overline{)354}\\-30\\\hline 54\\-54\\\hline 0\end{array}$
3 cannot be divided by 6, so look to the next digit. Think of a multiple of 6 that is near 35 but not greater than 35.	6 x 5 = 30	Subtract 30 from 35.	Bring the 4 down next to the 5. Now divide 54 by 6.	6 x 9 = 54 Write 9 in the ones place.

WRITE each quotient.

1. $6\overline{)174}$ 2. $8\overline{)416}$ 3. $5\overline{)310}$ 4. $3\overline{)297}$ 5. $7\overline{)238}$

6. $2\overline{)126}$ 7. $9\overline{)315}$ 8. $7\overline{)287}$ 9. $5\overline{)415}$ 10. $2\overline{)192}$

11. $7\overline{)567}$ 12. $8\overline{)640}$ 13. $4\overline{)312}$ 14. $9\overline{)513}$ 15. $3\overline{)372}$

Fact Finder

WRITE the quotient. Then WRITE two division problems and two multiplication problems for the three numbers.

Example:

$$5 \overline{)865} = 173$$

```
    173
5 ) 865
   -5
    36
   -35
    15
   -15
     0
```

865 ÷   5 = 173
865 ÷ 173 =   5
  5 × 173 = 865
173 ×   5 = 865

1. $6 \overline{)84}$

___ ÷ ___ = ___

___ ÷ ___ = ___

___ × ___ = ___

___ × ___ = ___

2. $2 \overline{)56}$

___ ÷ ___ = ___

___ ÷ ___ = ___

___ × ___ = ___

___ × ___ = ___

3. $9 \overline{)594}$

___ ÷ ___ = ___

___ ÷ ___ = ___

___ × ___ = ___

___ × ___ = ___

4. $7 \overline{)413}$

___ ÷ ___ = ___

___ ÷ ___ = ___

___ × ___ = ___

___ × ___ = ___

5. $4 \overline{)748}$

___ ÷ ___ = ___

___ ÷ ___ = ___

___ × ___ = ___

___ × ___ = ___

6. $3 \overline{)816}$

___ ÷ ___ = ___

___ ÷ ___ = ___

___ × ___ = ___

___ × ___ = ___

Computation Station

DIVIDE by a two-digit number.

HINT: Try writing multiples of the divisor before you begin.

Example:

| $12\overline{)552}$ | $\begin{array}{r} 4 \\ 12\overline{)552} \\ 48 \end{array}$ | $\begin{array}{r} 4 \\ 12\overline{)552} \\ -48 \\ \hline 7 \end{array}$ | $\begin{array}{r} 4 \\ 12\overline{)552} \\ -48 \\ \hline 72 \end{array}$ | $\begin{array}{r} 46 \\ 12\overline{)552} \\ -48 \\ \hline 72 \\ -72 \\ \hline 0 \end{array}$ |

WRITE each quotient.

1. $18\overline{)54}$ 2. $14\overline{)42}$ 3. $11\overline{)55}$ 4. $15\overline{)90}$ 5. $12\overline{)84}$

6. $16\overline{)192}$ 7. $24\overline{)480}$ 8. $37\overline{)592}$ 9. $17\overline{)663}$ 10. $25\overline{)375}$

11. $30\overline{)930}$ 12. $68\overline{)884}$ 13. $14\overline{)728}$ 14. $24\overline{)504}$ 15. $38\overline{)950}$

Computation Station

WRITE each quotient. Then MULTIPLY to check your work.

Example:

$$\begin{array}{r} 18 \\ 41{\overline{\smash{\big)}\,738}} \\ -41 \\ \hline 328 \\ -328 \\ \hline 0 \end{array}$$

$$\begin{array}{r} 18 \\ \times\,41 \\ \hline 18 \\ +720 \\ \hline 738 \end{array}$$

1. $22{\overline{\smash{\big)}\,616}}$ $\times\,22$

2. $64{\overline{\smash{\big)}\,704}}$ $\times\,64$

3. $12{\overline{\smash{\big)}\,432}}$ $\times\,12$

4. $30{\overline{\smash{\big)}\,630}}$ $\times\,30$

5. $34{\overline{\smash{\big)}\,510}}$ $\times\,34$

6. $14{\overline{\smash{\big)}\,728}}$ $\times\,14$

Any Way You Slice It

WRITE the fraction for each picture.

Example:

3 ← The **numerator** represents the number of shaded sections.

5 ← The **denominator** represents the total number of sections.

1. ___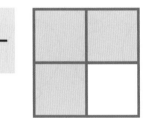

2. ___

3. ___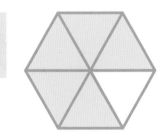

4. ___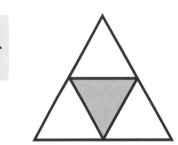

5. ___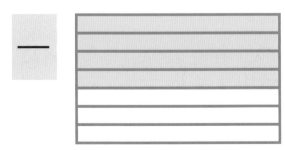

6. ___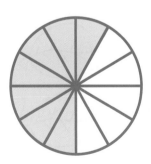

Recognizing Fractions

Color Sets

COLOR each set of pictures to match the fraction.

Example:

$\dfrac{4}{}$ ← The **numerator** represents the number of colored objects.

$\dfrac{}{7}$ ← The **denominator** represents the total number of objects.

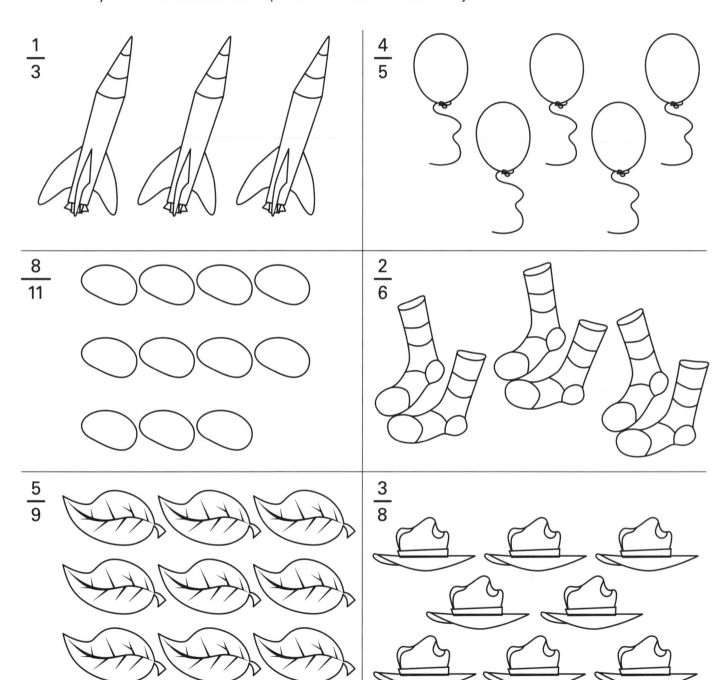

Color and Compare

COLOR the picture to match each fraction. Then CIRCLE the larger fraction.

$\dfrac{3}{4}$

$\dfrac{2}{5}$

$\dfrac{1}{6}$

$\dfrac{1}{3}$

$\dfrac{2}{3}$

$\dfrac{4}{8}$

$\dfrac{5}{6}$

$\dfrac{6}{7}$

$\dfrac{7}{12}$

$\dfrac{7}{9}$

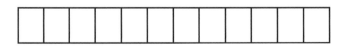

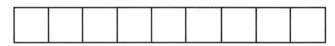

Matched or Mismatched?

WRITE >, <, or = in each box.

HINT: Fractions with larger denominators have smaller individual parts.

Example:

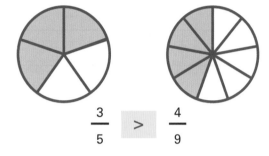

$$\frac{3}{5} \boxed{>} \frac{4}{9}$$

$\frac{3}{4} \boxed{} \frac{2}{4}$
1

$\frac{1}{7} \boxed{} \frac{7}{9}$
2

$\frac{3}{12} \boxed{} \frac{5}{8}$
3

$\frac{2}{5} \boxed{} \frac{1}{5}$
4

$\frac{6}{10} \boxed{} \frac{3}{10}$
5

$\frac{1}{2} \boxed{} \frac{4}{8}$
6

$\frac{6}{6} \boxed{} \frac{6}{9}$
7

$\frac{3}{7} \boxed{} \frac{8}{8}$
8

$\frac{1}{3} \boxed{} \frac{1}{4}$
9

$\frac{4}{6} \boxed{} \frac{11}{12}$
10

$\frac{2}{9} \boxed{} \frac{4}{5}$
11

$\frac{4}{9} \boxed{} \frac{3}{11}$
12

$\frac{3}{4} \boxed{} \frac{3}{5}$
13

$\frac{7}{11} \boxed{} \frac{7}{10}$
14

$\frac{6}{6} \boxed{} \frac{3}{3}$
15

$\frac{5}{2} \boxed{} \frac{2}{5}$
16

Fraction Circles

When fractions have the same denominator, add them by adding the numerators only. The denominator stays the same.

Example:

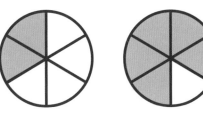

$$\frac{2}{6} + \frac{5}{6} = \frac{7}{6}$$

ADD the fractions and WRITE the sum.

1.
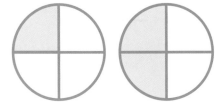

$$\frac{1}{4} + \frac{2}{4} = \underline{\quad}$$

2.

$$\frac{5}{9} + \frac{2}{9} = \underline{\quad}$$

3.
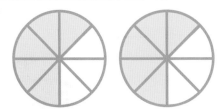

$$\frac{5}{8} + \frac{5}{8} = \underline{\quad}$$

4.
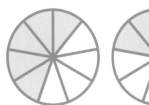

$$\frac{1}{7} + \frac{6}{7} = \underline{\quad}$$

5.
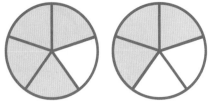

$$\frac{4}{5} + \frac{3}{5} = \underline{\quad}$$

6.

$$\frac{3}{6} + \frac{2}{6} = \underline{\quad}$$

More than One?

ADD the fractions. CIRCLE any sum that is greater than one.

HINT: A fraction is greater than one if the numerator is larger than the denominator.

1. $\dfrac{2}{6} + \dfrac{3}{6} = \dfrac{5}{6}$

2. $\dfrac{1}{3} + \dfrac{4}{3} = \underline{}$

3. $\dfrac{3}{10} + \dfrac{5}{10} = \underline{}$

4. $\dfrac{6}{9} + \dfrac{4}{9} = \underline{}$

5. $\dfrac{2}{7} + \dfrac{2}{7} = \underline{}$

6. $\dfrac{3}{5} + \dfrac{4}{5} = \underline{}$

7. $\dfrac{2}{4} + \dfrac{1}{4} = \underline{}$

8. $\dfrac{1}{2} + \dfrac{3}{2} = \underline{}$

9. $\dfrac{7}{12} + \dfrac{9}{12} = \underline{}$

10. $\dfrac{4}{6} + \dfrac{1}{6} = \underline{}$

11. $\dfrac{8}{11} + \dfrac{5}{11} = \underline{}$

12. $\dfrac{3}{8} + \dfrac{5}{8} = \underline{}$

Fraction Bars

When fractions have the same denominator, subtract them by subtracting the numerators only. The denominator stays the same.

Example:

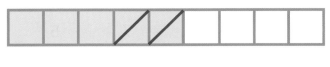

$$\frac{5}{9} - \frac{2}{9} = \frac{3}{9}$$

SUBTRACT the fractions and WRITE the difference.

HINT: Cross out the number of boxes of the second fraction to help you subtract.

1.

$$\frac{3}{4} - \frac{1}{4} = \underline{\quad}$$

2.

$$\frac{7}{8} - \frac{2}{8} = \underline{\quad}$$

3.

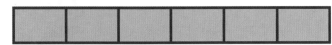

$$\frac{6}{6} - \frac{5}{6} = \underline{\quad}$$

4.

$$\frac{4}{5} - \frac{1}{5} = \underline{\quad}$$

5.

$$\frac{10}{12} - \frac{4}{12} = \underline{\quad}$$

6.

$$\frac{6}{7} - \frac{3}{7} = \underline{\quad}$$

Fraction Subtraction

WRITE each difference.

1. $\dfrac{4}{6} - \dfrac{3}{6} = $ —

2. $\dfrac{7}{8} - \dfrac{5}{8} = $ —

3. $\dfrac{2}{5} - \dfrac{1}{5} = $ —

4. $\dfrac{9}{10} - \dfrac{6}{10} = $ —

5. $\dfrac{5}{12} - \dfrac{2}{12} = $ —

6. $\dfrac{5}{7} - \dfrac{3}{7} = $ —

7. $\dfrac{8}{9} - \dfrac{4}{9} = $ —

8. $\dfrac{6}{4} - \dfrac{4}{4} = $ —

9. $\dfrac{8}{8} - \dfrac{2}{8} = $ —

10. $\dfrac{8}{5} - \dfrac{4}{5} = $ —

11. $\dfrac{5}{10} - \dfrac{1}{10} = $ —

12. $\dfrac{9}{6} - \dfrac{3}{6} = $ —

Tiny Tenths

This picture has $\frac{4}{10}$ shaded. In decimal form, this is written as 0.4.

ones	tenths
0	4

$\frac{4}{10}$ 0.4

WRITE the fraction and decimal for each picture.

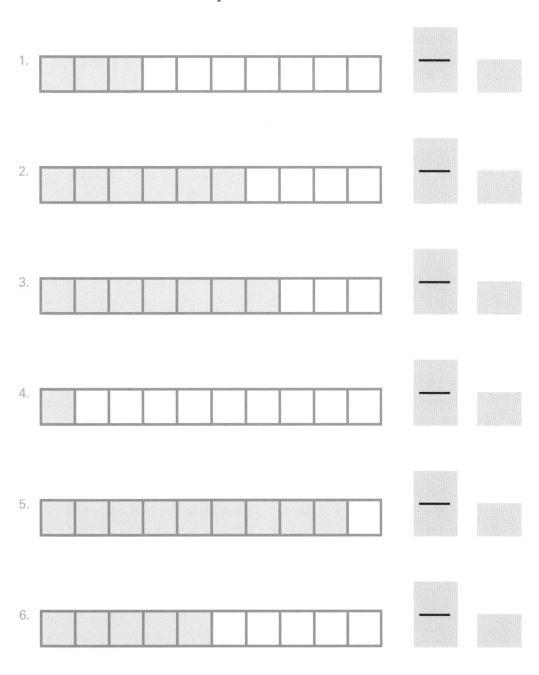

1.

2.

3.

4.

5.

6.

Handy Hundredths

This picture has $\frac{63}{100}$ shaded. In decimal form this is written as 0.63.

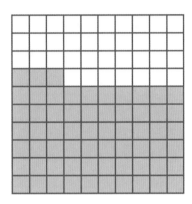

ones	tenths	hundredths
0	6	3

$\frac{63}{100}$

0.63

WRITE the fraction and decimal for each picture.

1.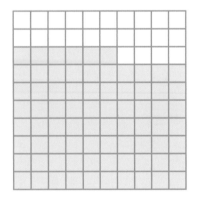

2.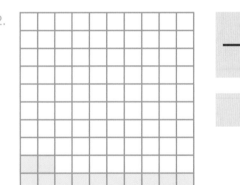

3.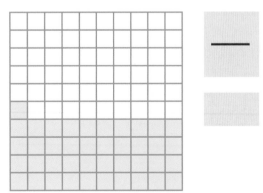

4.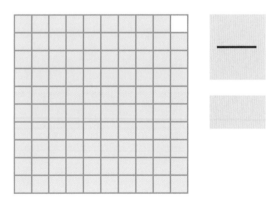

Cash Crunch

Decimals are used to represent dollars and cents. WRITE the value of the money in each row.

Example:

$6.38

1.

$ _____

2.

$ _____

3.

$ _____

4.

$ _____

5.

$ _____

Recognizing Decimals

Get in Line

WRITE the missing numbers in each number line.

1.

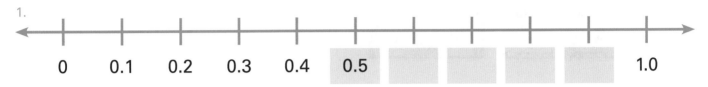

0   0.1   0.2   0.3   0.4   0.5   ☐   ☐   ☐   ☐   1.0

2.

2.0   ☐   2.2   ☐   2.4   ☐   2.6   2.7   ☐   2.9   ☐

3.

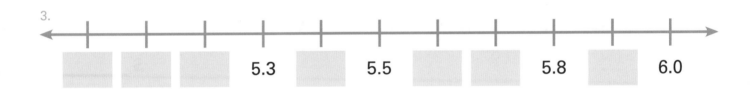

☐   ☐   ☐   5.3   ☐   5.5   ☐   ☐   5.8   ☐   6.0

4.

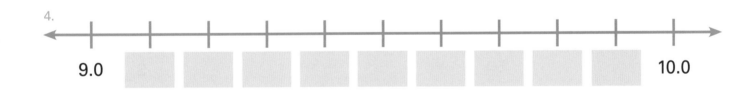

9.0   ☐   ☐   ☐   ☐   ☐   ☐   ☐   ☐   ☐   10.0

5.

3.3   3.4   ☐   3.6   ☐   3.9   ☐   4.1   ☐   4.3

6.

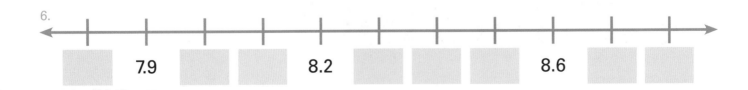

☐   7.9   ☐   8.2   ☐   ☐   8.6   ☐   ☐

Color and Compare

COLOR the picture to match each decimal. Then CIRCLE the smaller decimal.

0.5

0.3

0.2

0.8

0.9

0.7

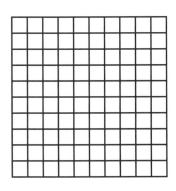

0.68

0.93

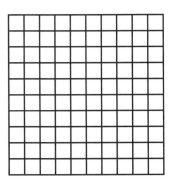

0.46

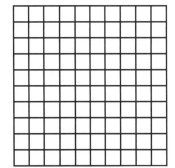

0.42

Matched or Mismatched?

COMPARE each pair of decimals, and WRITE >, <, or = in the box.

Example: 0.4 < 0.6

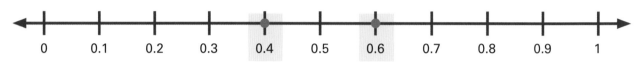

0.2 ☐ 0.8

0.6 ☐ 0.5

0.1 ☐ 0.2

0.4 ☐ 0.7

  1   2   3   4

1.4 ☐ 1.2

1.3 ☐ 1.7

1.8 ☐ 1.8

1.0 ☐ 0.9

  5   6   7   8

0.34 ☐ 0.27

0.42 ☐ 0.42

0.56 ☐ 0.61

0.92 ☐ 0.90

  9   10   11   12

1.55 ☐ 1.59

0.98 ☐ 1.89

0.76 ☐ 0.96

1.21 ☐ 1.21

  13   14   15   16

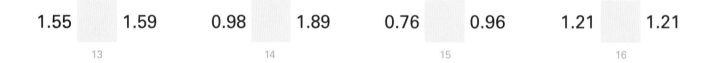

0.96 ☐ 1.26

1.45 ☐ 1.31

0.26 ☐ 0.25

1.02 ☐ 1.01

  17   18   19   20

Cash Crunch

ADD the dollar amounts.

Example: $10.54
            + 6.12

            $16.66

1. $14.63
    + 3.20

    $

2. $22.01
    + 5.78

    $

3. $44.82
    + 2.11

    $

4. $28.31
    +11.42

    $

5. $10.93
    +42.04

    $

6. $52.08
    +16.30

    $

7. $852.61
    + 13.14

    $

8. $162.20
    + 25.74

    $

9. $734.12
    + 51.40

    $

10. $418.16
    +150.03

    $

11. $331.04
    +311.24

    $

12. $243.24
    +753.21

    $

Adding & Subtracting Decimals

Cash Crunch

SUBTRACT the dollar amounts.

Example:

$21.57
−11.36
——
$10.21

1. $17.82
   − 2.51
   ————
   $

2. $64.32
   − 4.12
   ————
   $

3. $79.57
   − 8.21
   ————
   $

4. $31.99
   −20.96
   ————
   $

5. $13.84
   −10.72
   ————
   $

6. $81.76
   −41.06
   ————
   $

7. $368.62
   − 37.02
   ————
   $

8. $592.63
   − 71.42
   ————
   $

9. $454.66
   − 20.53
   ————
   $

10. $266.74
    −103.52
    ————
    $

11. $917.88
    −312.21
    ————
    $

12. $186.73
    −135.43
    ————
    $

It All Adds Up

When adding decimals, add and regroup as you normally would, keeping the decimal between the ones place and the tenths place.

¹ 53.85 + 67.56 ‾‾‾‾ 1 **Add the hundredths.** 5 + 6 = 11	¹ ¹ 53.85 + 67.56 ‾‾‾‾ .41 **Add the tenths.** 1 + 8 + 5 = 14	¹¹ ¹ 53.85 + 67.56 ‾‾‾‾ 1.41 **Add the ones.** 1 + 3 + 7 = 11	¹¹ ¹ 53.85 + 67.56 ‾‾‾‾ 121.41 **Add the tens.** 1 + 5 + 6 = 12

ADD each sum.

1.
$$7.5$$
$$+ \ 0.9$$

2.
$$3.21$$
$$+9.29$$

3.
$$81.94$$
$$+ \ 8.83$$

4.
$$28.53$$
$$+99.58$$

5.
$$11.76$$
$$+59.86$$

6.
$$27.36$$
$$+88.25$$

7.
$$575.07$$
$$+ \ 71.86$$

8.
$$448.86$$
$$+ \ 58.58$$

9.
$$199.69$$
$$+ \ 90.70$$

10.
$$197.45$$
$$+424.91$$

11.
$$514.37$$
$$+382.84$$

12.
$$347.79$$
$$+132.46$$

What's the Difference?

When subtracting decimals, subtract and regroup as you normally would, keeping the decimal between the ones place and the tenths place.

0 16 83.1̸6̸ − 16.37 9	2 10 16 8̸3̸.1̸6̸ − 16.37 .79	7 12 10 16 8̸3̸.1̸6̸ − 16.37 6.79	7 12 10 16 8̸3̸.1̸6̸ − 16.37 66.79
Subtract the hundredths. 16 − 7 = 9	Subtract the tenths. 10 − 3 = 7	Subtract the ones. 12 − 6 = 6	Subtract the tens. 7 − 1 = 6

WRITE each difference.

1.
$$6.4$$
$$-\ 3.5$$

2.
$$4.72$$
$$-1.16$$

3.
$$33.56$$
$$-\ 4.28$$

4.
$$52.1$$
$$-11.4$$

5.
$$63.18$$
$$-44.26$$

6.
$$32.37$$
$$-16.49$$

7.
$$848.08$$
$$-\ 77.41$$

8.
$$103.98$$
$$-\ 64.72$$

9.
$$282.45$$
$$-\ 53.94$$

10.
$$690.90$$
$$-131.45$$

11.
$$353.42$$
$$-262.24$$

12.
$$936.65$$
$$-573.79$$

Measure Up

MEASURE the length of each object in centimeters (cm).

1 centimeter is made up of 10 millimeters (mm).

Example: 3.2 cm

WRITE each answer as a decimal.

1. _____ cm

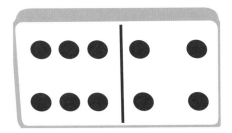

3. _____ cm

2. _____ cm

4. _____ cm

5. _____ cm

Preferred Measure

Which unit of measure would you use to measure the length of each object? WRITE *mm, cm, m,* or *km.*

1 centimeter (cm) = 10 millimeters (mm)

1 mm   1 cm

NOTE: These lines show how these units compare to each other. They are not actual size.

1 meter (m) = 100 centimeters

1 cm   1 m

1 kilometer (km) = 1,000 meters

1 m   1 km

1. Distance from Chicago to Toronto _____

2. Height of an adult _____

3. Length of a baby _____

4. Size of an ant _____

5. Distance of a 30-second run _____

6. Distance of a 30-minute run _____

7. Height of a basketball hoop _____

8. Size of a pencil _____

Measuring Mash-up

WRITE the equivalent measurement.

1 centimeter (cm) = 10 millimeters (mm)

1 meter (m) = 100 centimeters

1 kilometer (km) = 1,000 meters

Examples:

5 km = <u>5,000</u> m	1 kilometer = 1,000 meters	5 × 1,000 = 5,000
300 cm = <u>3</u> m	100 centimeters = 1 meter	300 ÷ 100 = 3

1. 6 m = _____ cm

2. 12 cm = _____ mm

3. 10 km = _____ m

4. 30 mm = _____ cm

5. 2,500 cm = _____ m

6. 25 cm = _____ mm

7. 6,000 m = _____ km

8. 46 m = _____ cm

9. 90 mm = _____ cm

10. 50 cm = _____ m

11. 8 mm = _____ cm

12. $\frac{1}{2}$ km = _____ m

Length

What's Longest?

CIRCLE the longest measurement in each row.

1 centimeter (cm) = 10 millimeters (mm)

1 meter (m) = 100 centimeters

1 kilometer (km) = 1,000 meters

1.	1 m	1 cm	1 km	1 mm
2.	14 mm	2 m	7 cm	5 cm
3.	1 m	200 cm	250 mm	96 cm
4.	40 m	4,000 mm	400 cm	4 mm
5.	2 km	2,500 cm	25 mm	2,500 m
6.	400 cm	5 m	6,000 mm	3 m

Measure Up

MEASURE the length of each object in inches (in.). WRITE each answer as a fraction.

$\frac{1}{4}$ $\frac{1}{2}$ $\frac{3}{4}$

1

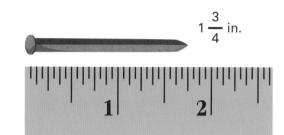

$1\frac{3}{4}$ in.

1 2

1. _____ in.

2. _____ in.

3. _____ in.

4. _____ in.

5. _____ in.

Preferred Measure

Which unit of measure would you use to measure the length of each object? WRITE *in.*, *ft*, *yd*, or *mi*.

1 foot (ft) = 12 inches

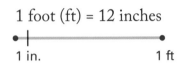

NOTE: These lines show how these units compare to each other. They are not actual size.

1 yard (yd) = 3 feet

1 mile (mi) = 1,760 yards or 5,280 feet

1 yd ──────────────────────────────────── 1 mi

1. Height of a coffee mug _____

2. Length of a football field _____

3. Height of a room _____

4. Distance from New York to Los Angeles _____

5. Length of a caterpillar _____

6. Distance across a small lake _____

7. Distance across the Pacific Ocean _____

8. Depth of a swimming pool _____

Measuring Mash-up

WRITE the equivalent measurement.

1 foot (ft) = 12 inches

1 yard (yd) = 3 feet

1 mile (mi) = 1,760 yards or 5,280 feet

Examples:

15 yd = _45_ ft

24 in. = _2_ ft

1 yard = 3 feet

12 inches = 1 foot

$15 \times 3 = 45$

$24 \div 12 = 2$

1. 2 ft = _____ in.

2. 36 in. = _____ ft

3. 1 yd = _____ in.

4. 3 mi = _____ yd

5. 24 yd = _____ ft

6. 3,520 yd = _____ mi

7. 52 ft = _____ in.

8. 2 mi = _____ ft

9. 336 in. = _____ ft

10. 72 in. = _____ yd

11. 6 in. = _____ ft

12. 1 ft = _____ yd

What's the Shortest?

CIRCLE the shortest measurement in each row.

1 foot (ft) = 12 inches

1 yard (yd) = 3 feet

1 mile (mi) = 1,760 yards or 5,280 feet

1.	1 mi	1 in.	1 yd	1 ft
2.	4 yd	5 mi	2 ft	26 in.
3.	40 in.	3 yd	2 mi	16 ft
4.	2,000 yd	1 mi	6,200 ft	1,729 yd
5.	180 in.	16 ft	6 yd	21 ft
6.	41 yd	6 mi	1, 445 in.	120 ft

Squared Away

Perimeter is the distance around a two-dimensional shape. **Area** is the size of the surface of a shape, and it is measured in square units.

To measure the **perimeter**, count the number of units on the outside of the rectangle.

To measure the **area**, count the number of square units.

The perimeter of this rectangle is 10 units.

The area of this rectangle is 6 square units.

1 square unit

WRITE the perimeter and area of each shape.

1.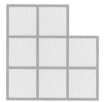

Perimeter: _____ units

Area: _____ square units

2.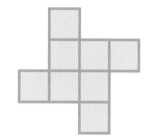

Perimeter: _____ units

Area: _____ square units

3.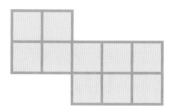

Perimeter: _____ units

Area: _____ square units

4.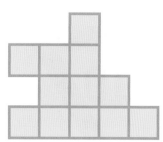

Perimeter: _____ units

Area: _____ square units

Around We Go

Find the perimeter by adding the length of every side.

30 in.

24 in.

24 + 30 + 24 + 30 = 108 in.

WRITE the perimeter of each shape.

10 in.

1. _____ in.

5 in. MAIN STREET

24 in.

2. _____ in.

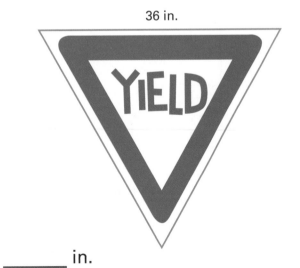

36 in.

12 in.

36 in.

3. _____ in.

4. _____ in.

Frame Up

Find the area of a rectangle by multiplying the length by the width. WRITE the area of each shape.

Example: 18 cm × 23 cm = 414 square centimeters (sq cm)

15 cm

10 cm

1. _____ sq cm

19 cm

24 cm

2. _____ sq cm

46 cm

36 cm

3. _____ sq cm

16 cm

16 cm

4. _____ sq cm

Rulers Rule

MEASURE each rectangle in centimeters. WRITE the perimeter and area of each shape.

1.

Perimeter: _____ cm

Area: _____ sq cm

2.

Perimeter: _____ cm

Area: _____ sq cm

3.

Perimeter: _____ cm

Area: _____ sq cm

Preferred Measure

Which unit of measure would you use to measure the weight of each object?
WRITE *oz*, *lb*, or *T*.

Examples:

1 ounce (oz)

1 pound (lb)
1 pound = 16 ounces

1 ton (T)
1 ton = 2,000 pounds

1. Weight of a hippopotamus _____

2. Weight of a person _____

3. Weight of a box of macaroni and cheese _____

4. Weight of a dump truck _____

5. Weight of a lemon _____

6. Weight of a bag of groceries _____

7. Weight of a sailboat _____

8. Weight of a plate _____

Weigh In

Each weight is shown in pounds. WRITE each weight in ounces.

HINT: One pound equals 16 ounces, so multiply each weight by 16.

_____ OZ

1

_____ OZ

2

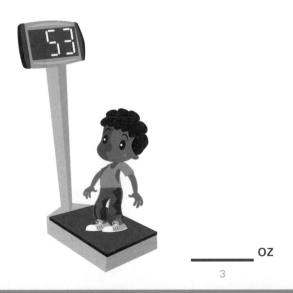

_____ OZ

3

_____ OZ

4

Measuring Mash-up

WRITE the equivalent measurement.

    1 pound (lb) = 16 ounces (oz)

    1 ton (T) = 2,000 pounds

Examples:

    3 T = <u>6,000</u> lb   1 ton = 2,000 pounds   3 × 2,000 = 6,000

    48 oz = <u>3</u> lb   16 ounces = 1 pound   48 ÷ 16 = 3

1. 32 oz = _____ lb

2. 4,000 lb = _____ T

3. 14 lb = _____ oz

4. 4 T = _____ lb

5. 50 lb = _____ oz

6. 192 oz = _____ lb

7. 20,000 lb = _____ T

8. 6 T = _____ lb

9. 100 lb = _____ oz

10. $\frac{1}{2}$ T = _____ lb

11. $\frac{1}{4}$ lb = _____ oz

12. $\frac{1}{2}$ lb = _____ oz

The Mighty Marlock

The Mighty Marlock will guess any weight, but he sometimes guesses incorrectly. CROSS OUT any picture where his guess is likely wrong.

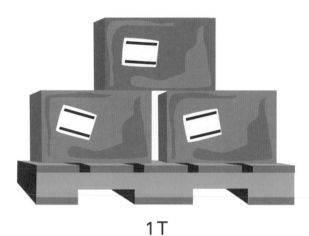

1 T

12 oz

6 oz

4 T

300 lb

8 lb

Preferred Measure

Which unit of measure would you use to measure the weight of each object? WRITE *mg, g,* or *kg.*

1 gram = 1,000 milligrams

1 kilogram = 1,000 grams

Examples:

1 milligram (1 mg)

1 gram (1 g)

1 kilogram (1 kg)

1. Weight of a pen _____

2. Weight of a lion _____

3. Weight of some sugar crystals _____

4. Weight of a sugar cube _____

5. Weight of a baby _____

6. Weight of a small piece of yarn _____

7. Weight of a remote control _____

8. Weight of a toothbrush _____

Weigh In

Each weight is shown in kilograms. WRITE each weight in grams.

1 kilogram = 1,000 grams

0.5 kilograms = 500 grams

0.1 kilograms = 100 grams

_____ g
1

_____ g
2

_____ g
3

_____ g
4

Measuring Mash-up

WRITE the equivalent measurement.

1 gram (g) = 1,000 milligrams (mg)

1 kilogram (kg) = 1,000 grams

Examples:

4 kg = __4,000__ g   1 kilogram = 1,000 grams   4 × 1,000 = 4,000

3,000 mg = __3__ g   1,000 milligrams = 1 gram   3,000 ÷ 1,000 = 3

1. 2 kg = _____ g

2. 6,000 g = _____ kg

3. 2,000 mg = _____ g

4. 0.1 kg = _____ g

5. 12 g = _____ mg

6. 10,000 g = _____ kg

7. 5,000 mg = _____ g

8. 0.5 g = _____ mg

9. 600 g = _____ kg

10. 400 g = _____ kg

11. 100 mg = _____ g

12. 2.3 kg = _____ g

The Mighty Marlock

The Mighty Marlock will guess any weight, but he sometimes guesses incorrectly. CROSS OUT any picture where his guess is likely wrong.

3 g

800 mg

7 mg

5 kg

75 g

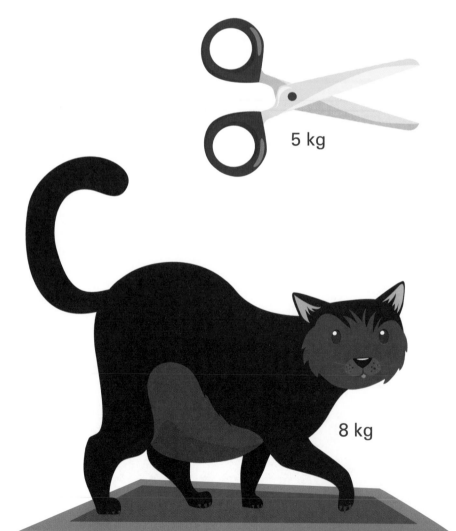

8 kg

Angle Untangle

An **angle** is formed when two lines meet, and it is measured in degrees using a protractor. There are three different types of angles: right, acute, and obtuse.

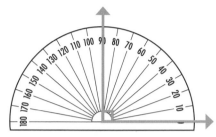 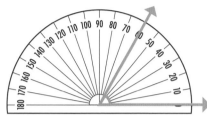 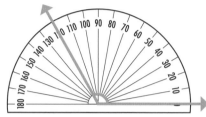

A **right** angle is an angle measuring exactly 90°, indicated by the ⌐ symbol in the corner.

An **acute** angle is any angle measuring less than 90°.

An **obtuse** angle is any angle measuring more than 90°.

WRITE *right*, *acute*, or *obtuse* for each angle.

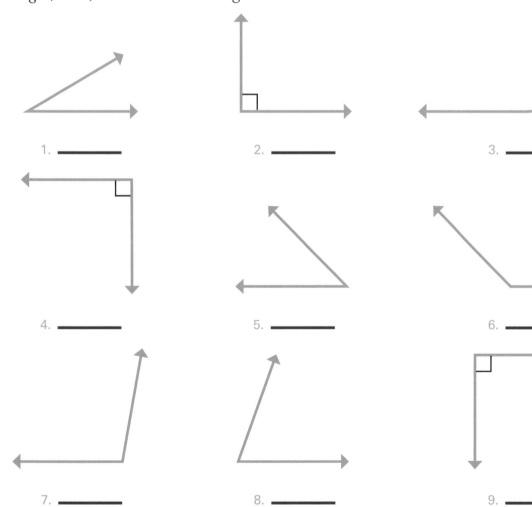

1. _____

2. _____

3. _____

4. _____

5. _____

6. _____

7. _____

8. _____

9. _____

Angles

Circle the Same

CIRCLE all of the angles that are in the correct column.

Right	Acute	Obtuse

What's My Name?

A **polygon** is a closed plane shape that has three or more sides. Polygons are named according to their number of sides.

 A **triangle** has three sides.

 A **rectangle** has four sides.

 A **square** is a special kind of rectangle that has four equal sides.

 A **pentagon** has five sides.

 A **hexagon** has six sides.

 A **heptagon** has seven sides.

 An **octagon** has eight sides.

 A **nonagon** has nine sides.

WRITE the name of each polygon.

1. _____

2. _____

3. _____

4. _____

5. _____

6. _____

7. _____

8. _____

Match Up

WRITE number of sides inside each polygon. Then DRAW a line to match each polygon to the correct name.

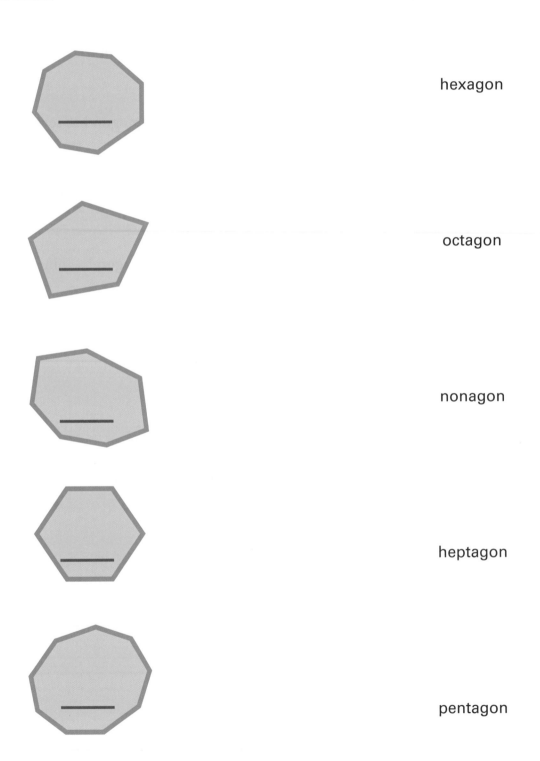

hexagon

octagon

nonagon

heptagon

pentagon

Polygon Pairs

COLOR all of the polygons in each row that match the word.

pentagon

   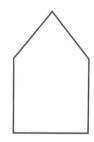

hexagon

 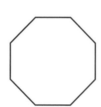 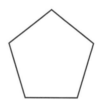 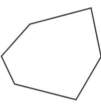

rectangle

nonagon

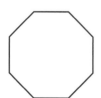 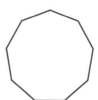 

Shape Up

A **vertex** is the point where two sides meet. A triangle has three vertices.

Example:

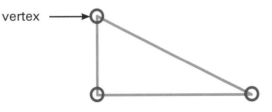

WRITE the name of each shape, the number of sides, and the number of vertices.

	Shape Name	Number of Sides	Number of Vertices

Hidden Angles

Two lines connected by a vertex form an angle. A square has four right angles.

WRITE the number of right, acute, and obtuse angles in each shape.

	Right Angles	Acute Angles	Obtuse Angles

Mystery Shape

WRITE the number of the mystery shape.

I have no right angles.

I have more vertices than the other shapes in my row.

I have seven sides.

Who am I? _____

Write It

Solid shapes are three-dimensional shapes.

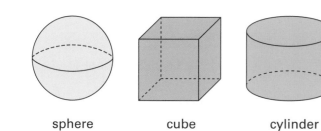 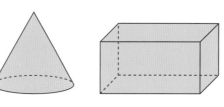 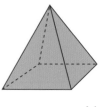

| sphere | cube | cylinder | cone | rectangular prism | square pyramid |

WRITE the name of each shape.

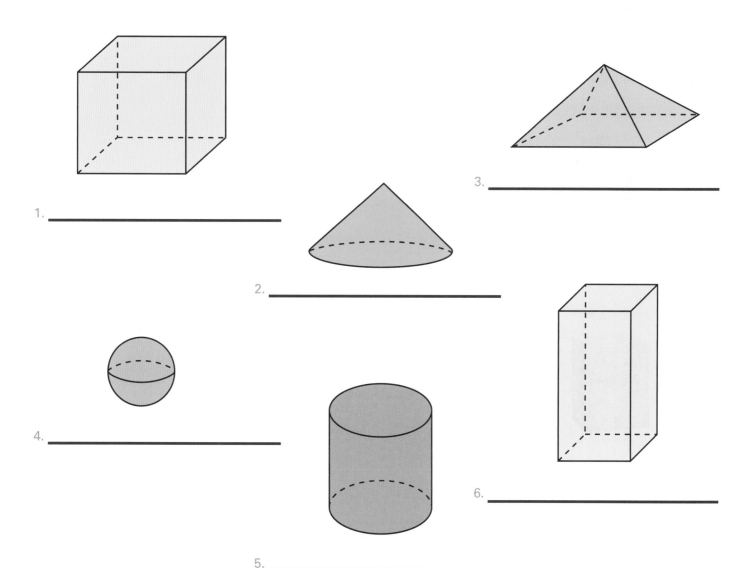

1. _____

2. _____

3. _____

4. _____

5. _____

6. _____

Match Up

DRAW a line to match each object with the correct shape name.

rectangular prism

cylinder

cone

cube

sphere

Shape Up

In a three-dimensional shape, a **vertex** is where three or more edges meet. An **edge** is where two sides meet. A **face** is the shape formed by the edges.

Example:

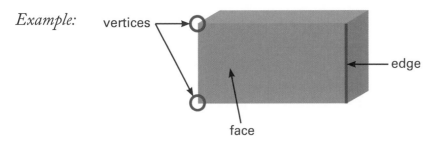

vertices

edge

face

WRITE the name of each shape and the number of vertices, edges, and faces it has.

	Shape Name	Number of Vertices	Number of Edges	Number of Faces

About Face

DRAW all of the shapes that are faces on each three-dimensional shape.

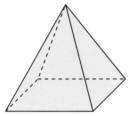 

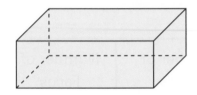

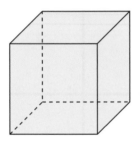

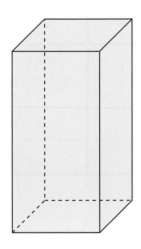

Find the Same

CIRCLE the object in each row that is the same shape as the first shape.

1.

2.

3.

4.

Mystery Shape

WRITE the number of the mystery shape.

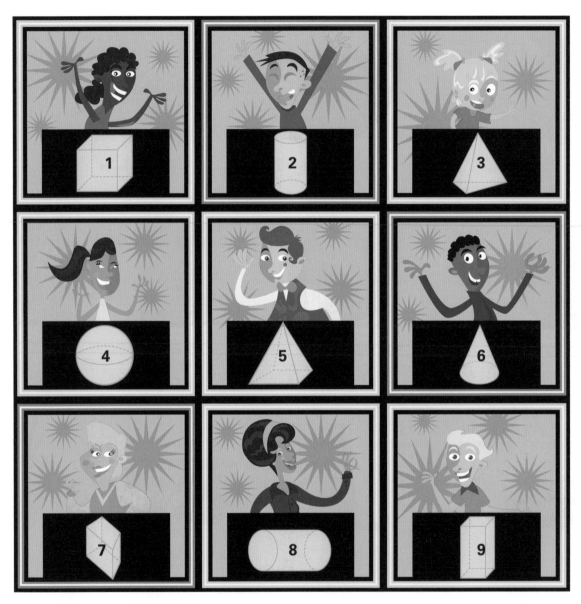

At least one of my faces is a square.

I have more than five vertices.

All of my edges are the same length.

Who am I? _____

Circle the Same

Intersecting lines are lines that cross one another.

Perpendicular lines intersect to form right angles.

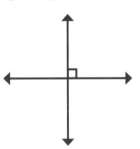

Parallel lines never intersect and are always the same distance apart.

CIRCLE all of the angles that match the word.

Intersecting	Perpendicular	Parallel

Lines in Shapes

Lines that form shapes can often be perpendicular or parallel.

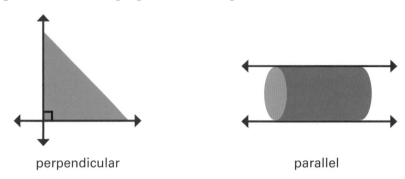

perpendicular   parallel

CIRCLE all of the shapes that have at least one pair of perpendicular lines.

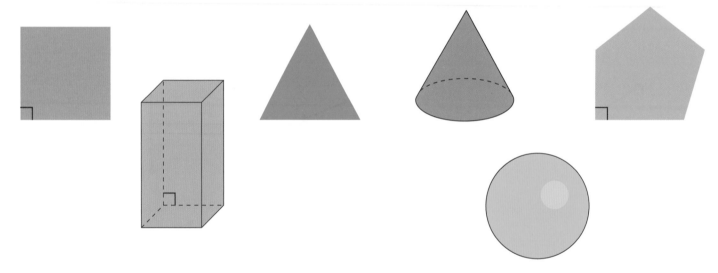

CIRCLE all of the shapes that have at least one pair of parallel lines.

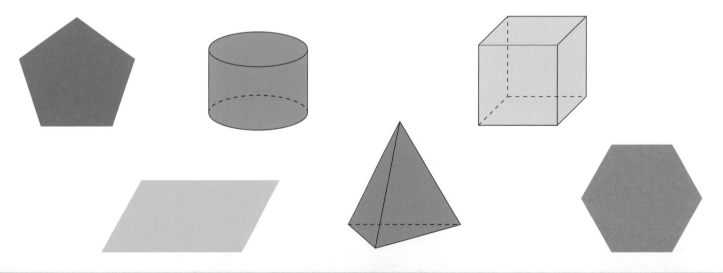

Any Which Way

A **flip**, **slide**, or **turn** has been applied to each shape. WRITE *flip*, *slide*, or *turn* on the line.

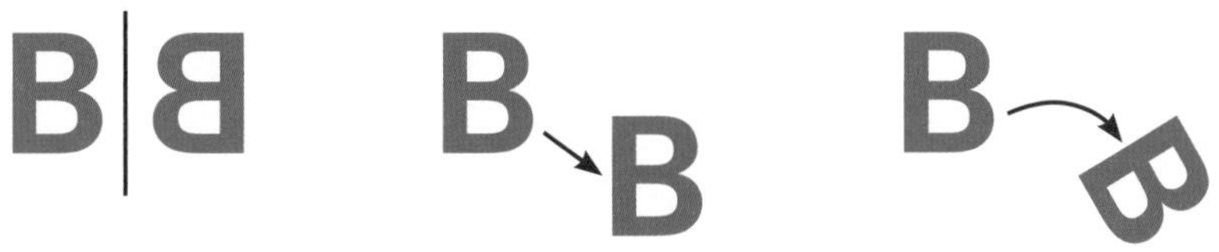

B|B
flip

B→B
slide

B↷B
turn

1. _____

A A

2. _____

W M

3. _____

X X

4. _____

Z Z

5. _____

R Я

6. _____

T T

7. _____

S S

8. _____

N N

Perfect Patterns

A **tessellation** is a repeating pattern of shapes that has no gaps or overlapping shapes. DRAW and COLOR the rest of each tessellation.

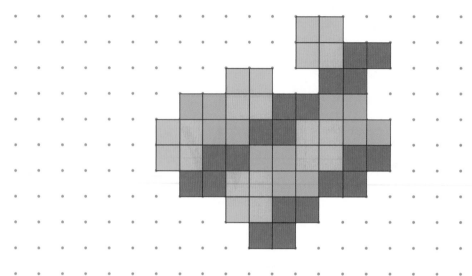

Answers

Page 3
1. two thousand, four hundred thirty-nine
2. forty-one thousand, five hundred eighty-two
3. seven hundred thirty-six thousand, one hundred twenty
4. five million, eight hundred twenty-four thousand, four hundred sixteen
5. nine million, three hundred one thousand, five hundred fifty-eight

Page 4
1. 6,942   2. 564,181
3. 2,223,846 4. 90,337
5. 4,119,673 6. 7,314
7. 1,882,450 8. 76,508
9. 230,729   10. 7,491,277

Page 5
1. 8, 5, 2, 3, 7, 6, 2
2. 1, 9, 9, 4, 8, 5, 7
3. 4, 3, 7, 0, 2, 8, 4
4. 6, 2, 5, 1, 3, 1, 9
5. 7, 8, 4, 2, 5, 2, 3
6. 5, 7, 1, 9, 6, 8, 8

Page 6
1. hundred thousands
2. thousands
3. millions
4. tens
5. ten thousands
6. ones
7. hundred thousands
8. hundreds

Page 7
1. > 2. > 3. < 4. <
5. > 6. > 7. > 8. >
9. < 10. < 11. < 12. >
13. > 14. > 15. > 16. <

Page 8
1. < 2. > 3. = 4. >
5. < 6. < 7. = 8. <
9. < 10. > 11. < 12. >
13. < 14. = 15. < 16. >

Page 9
1. 6,874   2. 11,160
3. 28,879   4. 680,391
5. 3,186,797 6. 7,198,003

Page 10
1. 3,420   2. 14,238
3. 45,297   4. 852,268
5. 4,163,588 6. 6,267,828

Page 11
1. 1,000   2. 8,000
3. 6,000   4. 9,000
5. 3,000   6. 5,000
7. 9,000   8. 5,000
9. 5,000   10. 80,000
11. 20,000   12. 20,000
13. 60,000   14. 60,000
15. 70,000   16. 20,000
17. 40,000   18. 30,000

Page 12
1. 700,000   2. 600,000
3. 100,000   4. 400,000
5. 200,000   6. 1,000,000
7. 400,000   8. 600,000
9. 3,000,000 10. 9,000,000
11. 5,000,000 12. 7,000,000
13. 5,000,000 14. 1,000,000
15. 3,000,000 16. 6,000,000

Page 13
Check: 561

Page 14

Page 15
1. 87,968   2. 17,456
3. 53,955   4. 29,684
5. 58,715   6. 94,597
7. 26,193   8. 79,264
9. 40,236   10. 84,753
11. 65,642   12. 59,695

Page 16
1. 78,583   2. 64,778
3. 90,960   4. 73,091
5. 47,226   6. 99,629
7. 26,038   8. 89,465

Pages 17
1. 50,182   2. 41,409
3. 92,328   4. 76,243
5. 69,021   6. 98,040
7. 33,149   8. 55,331
9. 78,013   10. 89,238
11. 63,082   12. 42,822

Pages 18
1. 14,224   2. 15,105
3. 19,947   4. 18,362
5. 43,979   6. 55,728
7. 65,632   8. 96,099
9. 34,500   10. 86,934
11. 91,536   12. 59,881

Page 19
1. 21,721   2. 53,036
3. 93,433   4. 77,102
5. 13,129   6. 51,213
7. 61,405   8. 43,524
9. 5,328   10. 22,740
11. 14,625   12. 39,351

Page 20
1. 43,587   2. 7,867
3. 57,872   4. 69,609
5. 25,558   6. 48,785
7. 6,347   8. 49,451
9. 75,135   10. 14,783
11. 29,977   12. 23,182

Page 21
1. 37,325   2. 65,529
3. 28,737   4. 43,556
5. 4,815   6. 57,763
7. 25,438   8. 11,936
9. 85,628   10. 27,830
11. 39,669   12. 13,612

Page 22
1. 37,434   2. 62,507
3. 77,128   4. 89,314
5. 88,677   6. 17,636
7. 14,283   8. 51,491
9. 25,849   10. 32,586
11. 11,977   12. 2,013
13. 40,368   14. 30,817
15. 2,392   16. 7,887

Page 23
1. 8,576   8,000
   + 1,259   + 1,000
    9,835   9,000

2. 9,662   9,000
   − 2,314   − 2,000
    7,348   7,000

3. 30,862   30,000
   + 2,775   + 2,000
    33,637   32,000

4. 46,237   40,000
   − 4,669   − 4,000
    41,568   36,000

5. 40,927   40,000
   + 35,290   + 30,000
    76,217   70,000

6. 99,730   90,000
   − 57,594   − 50,000
    42,136   40,000

Page 24
1. 19,343   20,000
   + 40,489   + 40,000
    59,832   60,000

2. 53,677   50,000
   − 24,156   − 20,000
    29,521   30,000

3. 65,563   70,000
   + 12,498   + 10,000
    78,061   80,000

4. 79,432   80,000
   − 42,722   − 40,000
    36,710   40,000

5. 57,249   60,000
   + 28,501   + 30,000
    85,750   90,000

6. 64,205   60,000
   − 52,198   − 50,000
    12,007   10,000

Page 25

0	0	0	0	0	0	0	0	0	0	0
0	1	2	3	4	5	6	7	8	9	10
0	2	4	6	8	10	12	14	16	18	20
0	3	6	9	12	15	18	21	24	27	30
0	4	8	12	16	20	24	28	32	36	40
0	5	10	15	20	25	30	35	40	45	50
0	6	12	18	24	30	36	42	48	54	60
0	7	14	21	28	35	42	49	56	63	70
0	8	16	24	32	40	48	56	64	72	80
0	9	18	27	36	45	54	63	72	81	90
0	10	20	30	40	50	60	70	80	90	100

Page 26
1. 15   2. 72   3. 6
4. 14   5. 30   6. 36
7. 56   8. 0   9. 64
10. 10   11. 63   12. 100
13. 30   14. 3   15. 42
16. 36   17. 80   18. 25
19. 27   20. 0   21. 10
22. 81   23. 24   24. 18
25. 49   26. 20   27. 9
28. 7   29. 48   30. 16

Page 27
1. 424   2. 156   3. 336

Page 28
1. 162   2. 230   3. 434
4. 171   5. 92   6. 280

Page 29
1. 48   2. 79   3. 279
4. 88   5. 39   6. 248
7. 168   8. 186   9. 400
10. 128 11. 219 12. 140
13. 546 14. 126 15. 87
16. 360 17. 208 18. 355

Page 30
1. 114   2. 288   3. 648
4. 210   5. 352   6. 301
7. 208   8. 325   9. 264
10. 48   11. 329 12. 296
13. 306 14. 608 15. 114
16. 212 17. 693 18. 765

Page 31
1. 704   2. 1,752
3. 7,344   4. 852
5. 3,835   6. 2,065
7. 2,421   8. 910
9. 1,328   10. 675
11. 3,598   12. 2,430
13. 2,724   14. 1,126
15. 2,552   16. 1,360
17. 2,784   18. 1,782

Page 32
1. 3,640   2. 744
3. 2,072   4. 3,980
5. 1,134   6. 1,848
7. 4,018   8. 1,161
9. 8,298   10. 2,185

Page 33
1. 1,134   2. 540
3. 2,835   4. 2,220
5. 3,528   6. 4,928
7. 4,230   8. 625
9. 1,001   10. 6,324
11. 779   12. 2,688
13. 8,772   14. 18,428
15. 54,600   16. 14,952
17. 10,665   18. 79,622

Page 34
1. 884   2. 3,150
3. 1,887   4. 4,416
5. 1,088   6. 5,740
7. 4,169   8. 12,685
9. 48,716   10. 52,101

Answers

Page 35
5: 5, 1, 7, 4, 10, 3, 2, 6, 9, 8
3: 5, 9, 4, 1, 10, 6, 2, 8, 3, 7
8: 1, 6, 10, 5, 2, 3, 7, 9, 4, 8
4: 6, 10, 4, 5, 8, 2, 3, 7, 9, 1
7: 3, 9, 4, 8, 5, 10, 2, 1, 7, 6
9: 2, 10, 1, 6, 7, 3, 4, 8, 9, 5

Page 36
1. 2   2. 7   3. 10
4. 9   5. 9   6. 7
7. 8   8. 8   9. 9
10. 1   11. 3   12. 8
13. 9   14. 10   15. 5
16. 9   17. 5   18. 2
19. 7   20. 10   21. 8
22. 4   23. 1   24. 3
25. 4   26. 10   27. 4
28. 5   29. 5   30. 8
31. 8   32. 9

Page 37
1. 11   2. 12   3. 16
4. 4   5. 4

Page 38
1. 18   2. 21   3. 12
4. 21   5. 24   6. 11
7. 13   8. 46   9. 17
10. 32   11. 25   12. 27
13. 34   14. 13   15. 12
16. 11   17. 12   18. 49

Page 39
1. 29   2. 52   3. 62
4. 99   5. 34   6. 63
7. 35   8. 41   9. 83
10. 96   11. 81   12. 80
13. 78   14. 57   15. 124

Page 40
1. 14
$84 \div 6 = 14$
$84 \div 14 = 6$
$6 \times 14 = 84$
$14 \times 6 = 84$

2. 28
$56 \div 2 = 28$
$56 \div 28 = 2$
$2 \times 28 = 56$
$28 \times 2 = 56$

3. 66
$594 \div 9 = 66$
$594 \div 66 = 9$
$9 \times 66 = 594$
$66 \times 9 = 594$

4. 59
$413 \div 7 = 59$
$413 \div 59 = 7$
$7 \times 59 = 413$
$59 \times 7 = 413$

5. 187
$748 \div 4 = 187$
$748 \div 187 = 4$
$4 \times 187 = 748$
$187 \times 4 = 748$

6. 272
$816 \div 3 = 272$
$816 \div 272 = 3$
$3 \times 272 = 816$
$272 \times 3 = 816$

Page 41
1. 3   2. 3   3. 5
4. 6   5. 7   6. 12
7. 20   8. 16   9. 39
10. 15   11. 31   12. 13
13. 52   14. 21   15. 25

Page 42
1. $22\overline{)616}$ = 28 $\begin{array}{r} 28 \\ \times 22 \\ \hline 616 \end{array}$

2. $64\overline{)704}$ = 11 $\begin{array}{r} 11 \\ \times 64 \\ \hline 704 \end{array}$

3. $12\overline{)432}$ = 36 $\begin{array}{r} 36 \\ \times 12 \\ \hline 432 \end{array}$

4. $30\overline{)630}$ = 21 $\begin{array}{r} 21 \\ \times 30 \\ \hline 630 \end{array}$

5. $34\overline{)510}$ = 15 $\begin{array}{r} 15 \\ \times 34 \\ \hline 510 \end{array}$

6. $14\overline{)728}$ = 52 $\begin{array}{r} 52 \\ \times 14 \\ \hline 728 \end{array}$

Page 43
1. $\frac{3}{4}$ 2. $\frac{5}{10}$ 3. $\frac{5}{6}$
4. $\frac{1}{4}$ 5. $\frac{4}{7}$ 6. $\frac{7}{12}$

Page 44
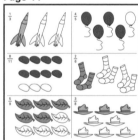

Page 45
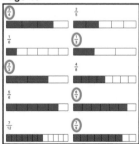

Page 46
1. >   2. <   3. <   4. >
5. >   6. =   7. >   8. <
9. >   10. <   11. <   12. >
13. >   14. <   15. =   16. >

Page 47
1. $\frac{3}{4}$ 2. $\frac{7}{9}$ 3. $\frac{10}{8}$
4. $\frac{7}{7}$ 5. $\frac{7}{5}$ 6. $\frac{5}{6}$

Page 48
1. $\frac{5}{6}$ 2. $\boxed{\frac{5}{3}}$ 3. $\frac{8}{10}$
4. $\boxed{\frac{10}{9}}$ 5. $\frac{4}{7}$ 6. $\boxed{\frac{7}{5}}$
7. $\frac{3}{4}$ 8. $\boxed{\frac{4}{2}}$ 9. $\boxed{\frac{16}{12}}$
10. $\frac{5}{6}$ 11. $\boxed{\frac{13}{11}}$ 12. $\frac{8}{8}$

Page 49
1. $\frac{2}{4}$ 2. $\frac{5}{8}$ 3. $\frac{1}{6}$
4. $\frac{3}{5}$ 5. $\frac{6}{12}$ 6. $\frac{3}{7}$

Page 50
1. $\frac{1}{6}$ 2. $\frac{2}{8}$ 3. $\frac{1}{5}$
4. $\frac{3}{10}$ 5. $\frac{3}{12}$ 6. $\frac{2}{7}$
7. $\frac{4}{9}$ 8. $\frac{2}{4}$ 9. $\frac{6}{8}$
10. $\frac{4}{5}$ 11. $\frac{4}{10}$ 12. $\frac{6}{6}$

Page 51
1. $\frac{3}{10}$, 0.3   2. $\frac{6}{10}$, 0.6
3. $\frac{7}{10}$, 0.7   4. $\frac{1}{10}$, 0.1
5. $\frac{9}{10}$, 0.9   6. $\frac{5}{10}$, 0.5

Page 52
1. $\frac{76}{100}$, 0.76   2. $\frac{12}{100}$, 0.12
3. $\frac{41}{100}$, 0.41   4. $\frac{99}{100}$, 0.99

Page 53
1. 1.48   2. 3.77   3. 5.67
4. 0.86   5. 7.09

Page 54
1. 0.5, 0.6, 0.7, 0.8, 0.9
2. 2.1, 2.3, 2.5, 2.8, 3.0
3. 5.0, 5.1, 5.2, 5.4, 5.6, 5.7, 5.9
4. 9.1, 9.2, 9.3, 9.4, 9.5, 9.6, 9.7, 9.8, 9.9
5. 3.5, 3.7, 3.8, 4.0, 4.2
6. 7.8, 8.0, 8.1, 8.3, 8.4, 8.5, 8.7, 8.8

Page 55
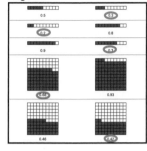

Page 56
1. <   2. >   3. <   4. <
5. >   6. <   7. =   8. >
9. >   10. =   11. <   12. >
13. <   14. <   15. <   16. =
17. <   18. >   19. >   20. >

Page 57
1. 17.83   2. 27.79
3. 46.93   4. 39.73
5. 52.97   6. 68.38
7. 865.75   8. 187.94
9. 785.52   10. 568.19
11. 642.28   12. 996.45

Page 58
1. 15.31   2. 60.20
3. 71.36   4. 11.03
5. 3.12   6. 40.70
7. 331.60   8. 521.21
9. 434.13   10. 163.22
11. 605.67   12. 51.30

Page 59
1. 8.4   2. 12.50
3. 90.77   4. 128.11
5. 71.62   6. 115.61
7. 646.93   8. 507.44
9. 290.39   10. 622.36
11. 897.21   12. 480.25

Page 60
1. 2.9   2. 3.56
3. 29.28   4. 40.7
5. 18.92   6. 15.88
7. 770.67   8. 39.26
9. 228.51   10. 559.45
11. 91.18   12. 362.86

Page 61
1. 2.3   2. 8.6   3. 5.6
4. 6.4   5. 15.6

Page 62
1. km   2. m   3. cm
4. mm   5. m   6. km
7. m   8. cm

Page 63
1. 600   2. 120   3. 10,000
4. 3   5. 25   6. 250
7. 6   8. 4,600   9. 9
10. 0.5   11. 0.8   12. 500

Page 64
1. 1 km   2. 2 m
3. 200 cm   4. 40 m
5. 2,500 m   6. 6,000 mm

Answers

Page 65

1. $1\frac{3}{4}$ 2. $3\frac{1}{2}$ 3. $\frac{3}{4}$

4. $2\frac{1}{4}$ 5. $6\frac{3}{4}$

Page 66
1. in. 2. yd
3. ft 4. mi
5. in. 6. yd
7. mi 8. ft

Page 67
1. 24 2. 3 3. 36
4. 5,280 5. 72 6. 2
7. 624 8. 10,560 9. 28

10. 2 11. $\frac{1}{2}$ 12. $\frac{1}{3}$

Page 68
1. 1 in. 2. 2 ft 3. 40 in.
4. 1,729 yd 5. 180 in. 6. 120 ft

Page 69
1. 12, 8 2. 16, 8
3. 16, 10 4. 20, 12

Page 70
1. 80 2. 58
3. 108 4. 96

Page 71
1. 150 2. 456
3. 1,656 4. 256

Page 72
1. 24, 32 2. 28, 49
3. 28, 45

Page 73
1. T 2. lb 3. oz 4. T
5. oz 6. lb 7. T 8. oz

Page 74
1. 2,336 2. 3,600
3. 848 4. 1,152

Page 75
1. 2 2. 2
3. 224 4. 8,000
5. 800 6. 12
7. 10 8. 12,000
9. 1,600 10. 1,000
11. 4 12. 8

Page 76

Page 77
1. g 2. kg 3. mg 4. g
5. kg 6. mg 7. g 8. g

Page 78
1. 1,100 2. 200
3. 600 4. 9,000

Page 79
1. 2,000 2. 6 3. 2
4. 100 5. 12,000 6. 10
7. 5 8. 500 9. 0.6
10. 0.4 11. 0.1 12. 2,300

Page 80

Page 81
1. acute 2. right 3. obtuse
4. right 5. acute 6. obtuse
7. obtuse 8. acute 9. right

Page 82
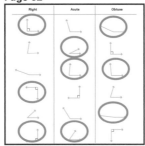

Page 83
1. pentagon
2. heptagon
3. square or rectangle
4. nonagon
5. octagon
6. triangle
7. rectangle
8. hexagon

Page 84
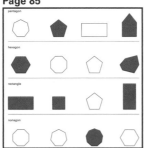

Page 85
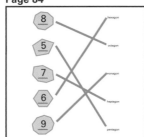

Page 86
pentagon 5 5
nonagon 9 9
rectangle 4 4
heptagon 7 7
hexagon 6 6
octagon 8 8

Page 87
4 0 0
0 2 2
1 2 0
0 0 9
2 1 2
0 3 0

Page 88
7

Page 89
1. cube
2. cone
3. square pyramid
4. sphere
5. cylinder
6. rectangular prism

Page 90
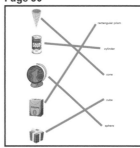

Page 91
cube 8 12 6
square pyramid 5 8 5
rectangular prism 8 12 6

Page 92
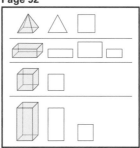

Page 93

Page 94
1

Page 95
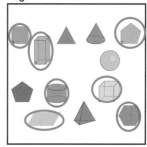

Page 96
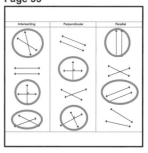

Page 97
1. turn 2. turn
3. slide 4. flip
5. flip 6. turn
7. turn 8. slide

Page 98
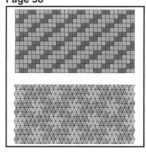

4th Grade
Math
Games & Puzzles

Number Search

WRITE each number. Then CIRCLE it in the puzzle.

HINT: Numbers are across and down only.

1. eighty-four thousand, one hundred sixty-five __84,165__

2. four million, six hundred seventy-two thousand, two hundred forty-four _____

3. nine hundred sixty-one thousand, seven hundred twenty-three _____

4. twenty-nine thousand, eight hundred eleven _____

5. one hundred fifteen thousand, seven hundred thirty-six _____

6. two million, eighty-two thousand, six hundred forty-one _____

7. five hundred five thousand, six hundred ninety-two _____

8. three million, nine hundred thirty-seven thousand, two hundred sixty _____

2	9	8	1	1	0	0	2
9	5	0	5	6	9	2	0
8	1	8	2	4	6	7	8
2	4	4	9	9	1	3	2
0	5	1	1	5	7	3	6
3	4	6	7	2	2	4	4
6	0	5	3	7	3	4	1
3	9	3	7	2	6	0	8

Criss Cross

READ the clues, and WRITE the numbers in the puzzle.

ACROSS

1. two million, five hundred ninety-one thousand, three hundred twenty-four

4. eight million, four hundred sixty-seven thousand, five hundred fifty-three

7. ninety-six thousand, eight hundred twenty-four

10. sixty-four thousand, one hundred ninety-nine

11. one million, one hundred fifty-two thousand, seven hundred three

14. two hundred seventy thousand, three hundred ninety-six

17. six hundred twenty-eight thousand, nine hundred thirty-one

DOWN

2. five hundred seventy-eight thousand, thirty-six

3. three hundred seven thousand, two hundred ninety-four

6. three million, seven hundred forty-two thousand, six hundred eighty

7. nine million, four hundred thirty-one thousand, fifty-two

8. eighty-eight thousand, seven hundred sixteen

9. four million, nine hundred thirteen thousand, five hundred forty-six

12. five million, six hundred nine thousand, four hundred twenty-eight

13. three hundred sixty-four thousand, seven hundred seventy-one

15. seventy-three thousand, nineteen

16. one hundred ninety-seven thousand, three hundred seven

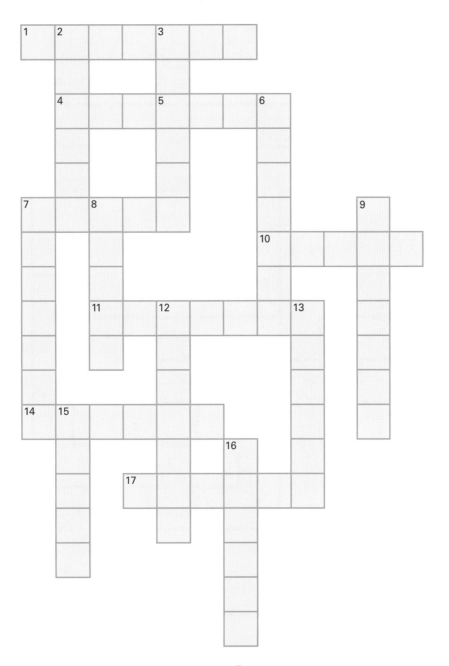

Place Value

Secret Number

DRAW a line to get from the start of the maze to the end without taking any extra paths. WRITE each number you cross in order, starting with the millions place, to find the secret number.

Secret number:
_____

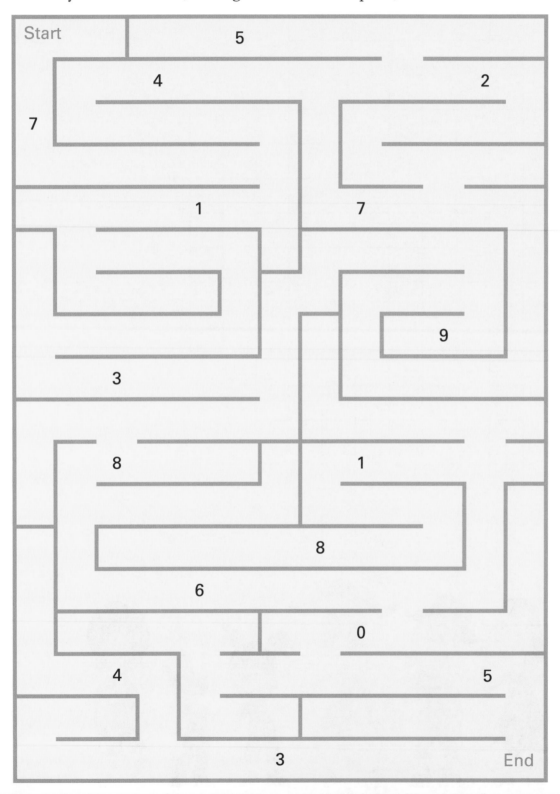

Totally Tangled

Each numbered circle is connected to another numbered circle. FIND the pairs of numbers, and COLOR any pair that shows a number with that number correctly rounded to the nearest ten thousand.

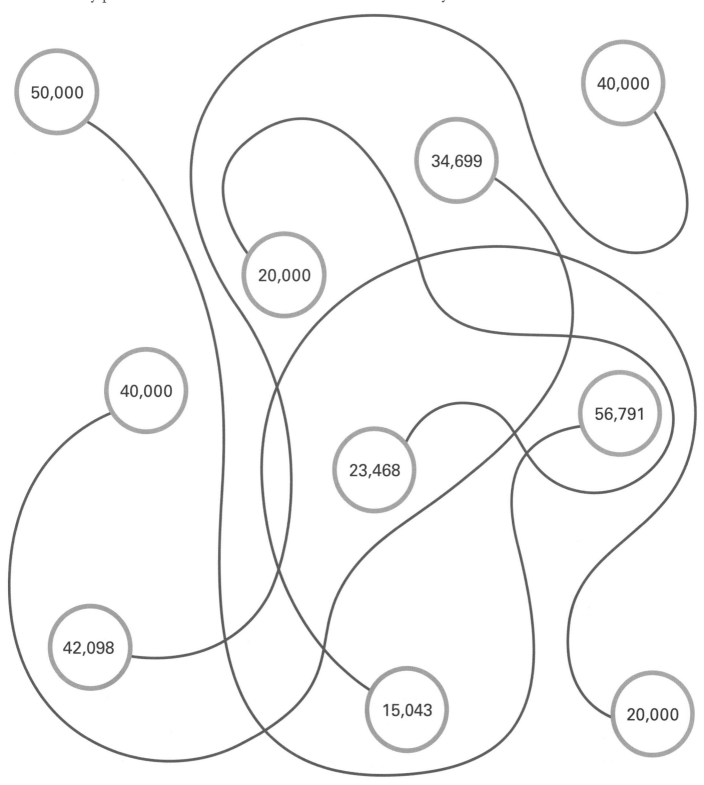

Just Right

WRITE each of the numbers to correctly complete the sentences.

HINT: There may be more than one place to put a number, but you need to use every number.

| 341,156 | 392,382 | 275,319 | 337,236 | 232,981 |
| 384,620 | 228,864 | 382,495 | 246,518 | |

1. _____ rounded to the nearest thousand is 229,000.

2. _____ rounded to the nearest ten thousand is 340,000.

3. _____ rounded to the nearest hundred thousand is 300,000.

4. _____rounded to the nearest ten thousand is 380,000.

5. _____ rounded to the nearest thousand is 382,000.

6. _____ rounded to the nearest hundred thousand is 400,000.

7. _____ rounded to the nearest ten thousand is 230,000.

8. _____ rounded to the nearest thousand is 337,000.

9. _____ rounded to the nearest hundred thousand is 200,000.

Picking Pairs

DRAW a line to connect each number with that number rounded to the nearest hundred thousand.

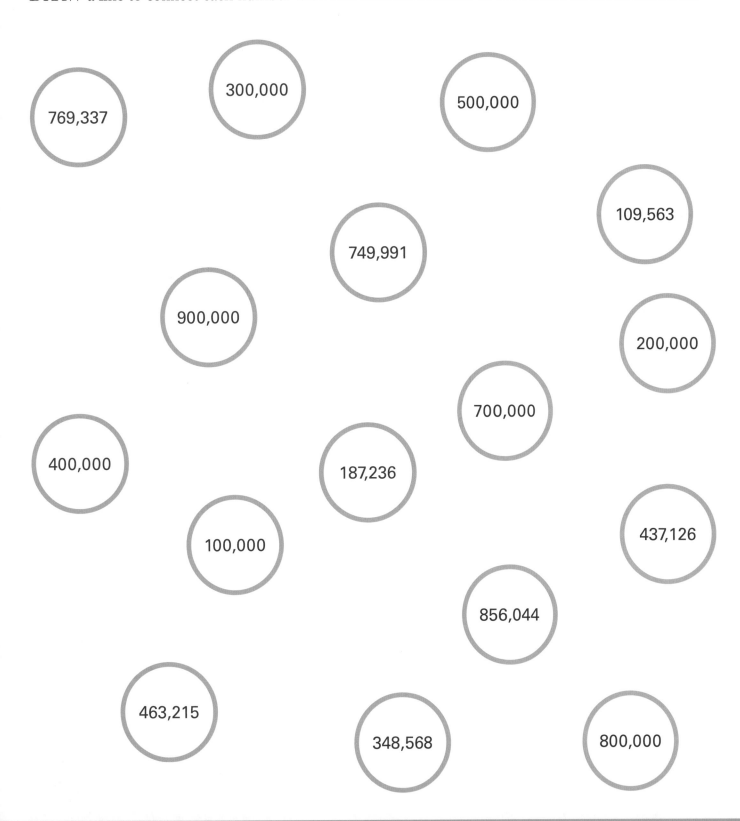

769,337

300,000

500,000

109,563

749,991

900,000

200,000

700,000

400,000

187,236

437,126

100,000

856,044

463,215

348,568

800,000

Just Right

WRITE each of the numbers to correctly complete the sentence.

HINT: There may be more than one place to put a number, but you need to use every number.

5,418,163	5,908,752	5,826,138	6,692,556	5,237,564
6,694,204	5,879,215	5,418,921	6,563,827	

1. _____ rounded to the nearest million is 5,000,000.

2. _____ rounded to the nearest hundred thousand is 5,400,000.

3. _____ rounded to the nearest ten thousand is 5,910,000.

4. _____ rounded to the nearest hundred thousand is 6,700,000.

5. _____ rounded to the nearest thousand is 6,694,000.

6. _____ rounded to the nearest million is 7,000,000.

7. _____ rounded to the nearest hundred thousand is 5,900,000.

8. _____ rounded to the nearest thousand is 5,419,000.

9. _____ rounded to the nearest million is 6,000,000.

Number Factory

WRITE the numbers that will come out of each machine.

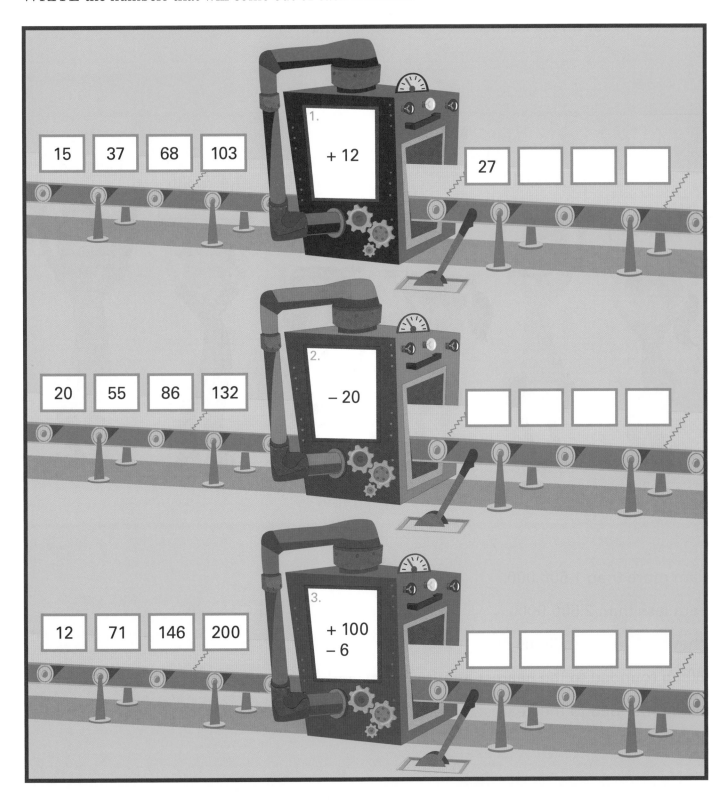

1. 15 37 68 103 + 12 27 ___ ___ ___

2. 20 55 86 132 − 20 ___ ___ ___ ___

3. 12 71 146 200 + 100 − 6 ___ ___ ___ ___

Who Am I?

READ the clues, and CIRCLE the mystery number.

HINT: Cross out any number that does not match the clues.

I am more than 1,500,000.

I am less than 2,500,000.

I have a 1 in the millions place.

When rounded to the nearest hundred thousand, I'm 1,800,000.

When rounded to the nearest ten thousand, I'm 1,840,000.

Who am I?

Number Factory

WRITE the numbers that will come out of each machine.

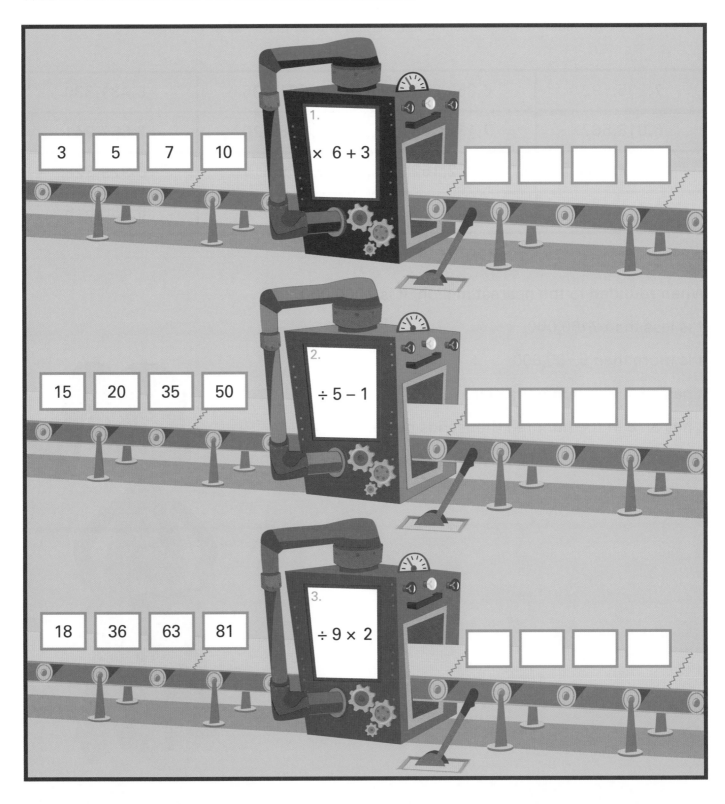

Last One Standing

CROSS OUT each number that does not match the clues until one number is left.

HINT: Follow the clues in order. The last number left should match all of the clues.

7,235,192	6,850,561	7,091,535	6,431,830
6,818,567	7,139,408	6,328,320	7,557,241
7,574,688	8,002,152	7,978,614	6,929,328
6,513,216	6,489,773	7,156,902	6,830,515

When rounded to the nearest million, it is 7,000,000.

It is less than 7,100,000.

It is more than 6,700,000.

It has a 5 in the hundreds place.

It has an 8 in the hundred thousands place.

When rounded to the nearest ten thousand, it is 6,820,000.

Pipe Down

WRITE the missing number. Then FOLLOW the pipe, and WRITE the same number in the next problem.

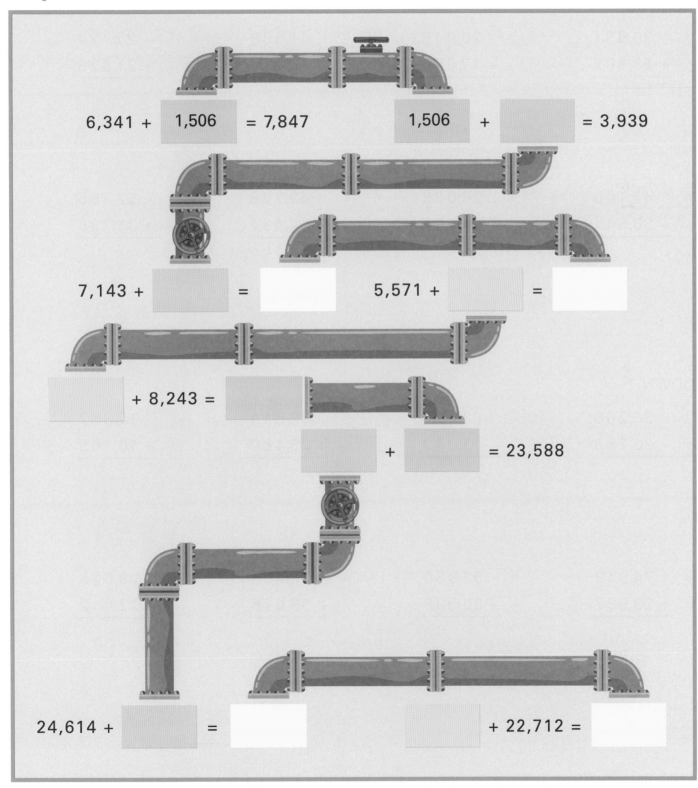

$6,341 +$ 1,506 $= 7,847$ 1,506 $+$ _____ $= 3,939$

$7,143 +$ _____ $=$ _____ 5,571 $+$ _____ $=$ _____

_____ $+ 8,243 =$ _____

_____ $+$ _____ $= 23,588$

$24,614 +$ _____ $=$ _____ _____ $+ 22,712 =$ _____

Adding

Criss Cross

SOLVE the addition problems, and WRITE the sums in the puzzle.

ACROSS

1. 36,981
  + 28,302

3. 20,046
  + 17,060

5. 41,989
  + 16,138

7. 27,724
  + 21,628

9. 42,105
  + 38,541

10. 26,028
  + 44,164

12. 43,778
  + 14,464

13. 52,995
  + 31,736

DOWN

1. 36,268
  + 33,286

2. 68,692
  + 13,043

4. 39,614
  + 25,460

6. 17,867
  + 10,165

8. 74,943
  + 23,987

9. 52,030
  + 30,938

10. 36,439
  + 35,675

11. 29,625
  + 22,812

Adding

Number Search

WRITE each sum. Then CIRCLE it in the puzzle.

HINT: Numbers are across and down only.

1.
   48,350
   + 28,627

2.
   16,129
   + 69,414

3.
   39,524
   + 11,825

4.
   36,942
   + 22,926

5.
   85,924
   + 13,834

6.
   46,561
   + 15,811

7.
   21,842
   + 18,861

8.
   43,527
   + 27,703

4	0	7	0	3	6	5	7
1	3	9	8	5	2	2	6
0	9	9	5	1	3	4	9
8	6	7	0	4	7	9	7
5	4	5	7	9	2	0	7
5	9	8	6	8	3	1	5
4	9	2	7	1	2	3	0
3	1	1	4	0	8	7	4

Pipe Down

WRITE the missing number. Then FOLLOW the pipe, and WRITE the same number in the next problem.

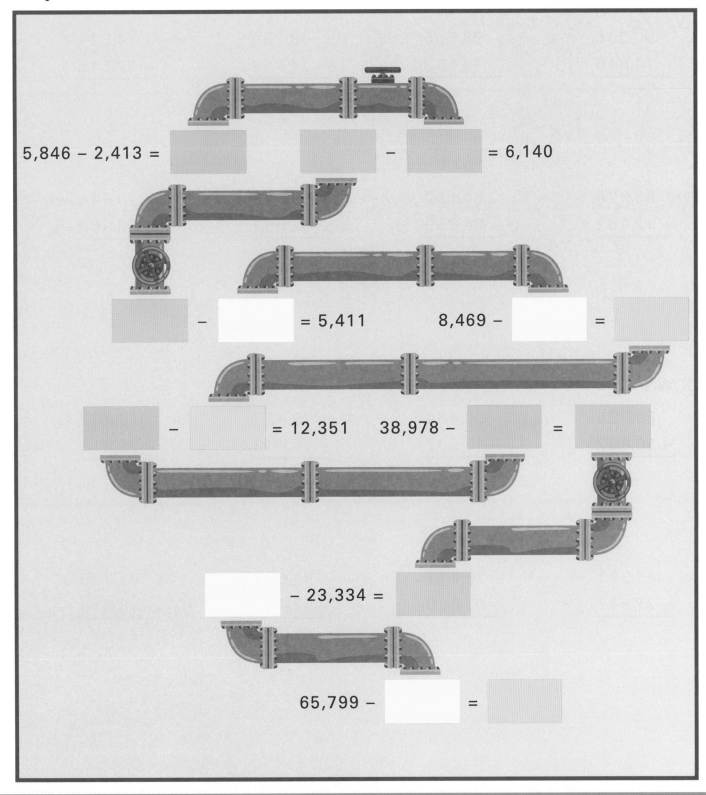

$$5{,}846 - 2{,}413 = \boxed{} \qquad \boxed{} - \boxed{} = 6{,}140$$

$$\boxed{} - \boxed{} = 5{,}411 \qquad 8{,}469 - \boxed{} = \boxed{}$$

$$\boxed{} - \boxed{} = 12{,}351 \qquad 38{,}978 - \boxed{} = \boxed{}$$

$$\boxed{} - 23{,}334 = \boxed{}$$

$$65{,}799 - \boxed{} = \boxed{}$$

Subtracting

Criss Cross

SOLVE the subtraction problems, and WRITE the differences in the puzzle.

ACROSS

1.
$$\begin{array}{r} 50,336 \\ -\ 14,845 \\ \hline \end{array}$$

5.
$$\begin{array}{r} 98,565 \\ -\ 18,133 \\ \hline \end{array}$$

7.
$$\begin{array}{r} 48,130 \\ -\ 24,154 \\ \hline \end{array}$$

9.
$$\begin{array}{r} 74,221 \\ -\ 52,516 \\ \hline \end{array}$$

10.
$$\begin{array}{r} 63,920 \\ -\ 12,462 \\ \hline \end{array}$$

11.
$$\begin{array}{r} 84,162 \\ -\ 35,059 \\ \hline \end{array}$$

15.
$$\begin{array}{r} 86,920 \\ -\ 62,591 \\ \hline \end{array}$$

16.
$$\begin{array}{r} 70,644 \\ -\ 43,969 \\ \hline \end{array}$$

DOWN

2.
$$\begin{array}{r} 89,299 \\ -\ 30,887 \\ \hline \end{array}$$

3.
$$\begin{array}{r} 26,604 \\ -\ 10,597 \\ \hline \end{array}$$

4.
$$\begin{array}{r} 79,867 \\ -\ 16,943 \\ \hline \end{array}$$

6.
$$\begin{array}{r} 43,837 \\ -\ 25,911 \\ \hline \end{array}$$

8.
$$\begin{array}{r} 63,391 \\ -\ 27,917 \\ \hline \end{array}$$

12.
$$\begin{array}{r} 76,012 \\ -\ 63,060 \\ \hline \end{array}$$

13.
$$\begin{array}{r} 90,653 \\ -\ 52,437 \\ \hline \end{array}$$

14.
$$\begin{array}{r} 81,033 \\ -\ 18,815 \\ \hline \end{array}$$

Number Search

WRITE each difference. Then CIRCLE it in the puzzle.

HINT: Numbers are across and down only.

1. 50,308
   − 27,997

2. 94,690
   − 18,477

3. 83,818
   − 28,594

4. 90,620
   − 19,602

5. 69,262
   − 19,386

6. 54,532
   − 36,296

7. 87,855
   − 26,769

8. 45,199
   − 10,227

1	8	2	3	6	9	6	1
7	6	2	4	6	0	1	7
1	1	0	2	3	5	0	1
3	5	5	2	2	4	8	0
4	2	2	3	5	9	6	1
9	0	4	1	6	8	1	8
7	6	2	1	3	7	6	2
2	9	8	8	3	6	7	2

Picking Pairs

ESTIMATE each sum or difference by rounding to the nearest ten thousand. DRAW a line to connect each problem with the correct estimate of the sum or difference.

30,000

32,199 + 29,486 =

11,375 + 8,268 =

40,000

58,659 − 23,926 =

10,000

81,292 − 65,653 =

19,410 + 12,342 =

60,000

92,084 − 37,241 =

50,000

20,000

Hidden Design

ESTIMATE each sum or difference by rounding each number to the nearest thousand. Then COLOR the squares that match the numbers to see the hidden design.

23,671 + 5,092 =   68,349 – 42,688 =   12,765 + 18,135 =

50,913 – 16,320 =   14,826 + 22,751 =   40,559 – 13,429 =

25,000	38,000	25,000	28,000	29,000	31,000	29,000	28,000
38,000	35,000	38,000	25,000	28,000	29,000	28,000	25,000
35,000	31,000	35,000	38,000	25,000	28,000	25,000	38,000
31,000	29,000	31,000	35,000	38,000	25,000	38,000	35,000
29,000	28,000	29,000	31,000	35,000	38,000	35,000	31,000
28,000	25,000	28,000	29,000	31,000	35,000	31,000	29,000
25,000	38,000	25,000	28,000	29,000	31,000	29,000	28,000
38,000	35,000	38,000	25,000	28,000	29,000	28,000	25,000

Code Breaker

SOLVE each problem. WRITE the letter that matches each product to solve the riddle.

6 × 5	8 × 2	9 × 4	5 × 5	3 × 8	1 0 × 6
1	2	3	4	5	6
M	R	W	U	V	H

7 × 1	9 × 8	6 × 8	2 × 9	9 × 5	1 0 × 4
7	8	9	10	11	12
Y	E	P	T	O	I

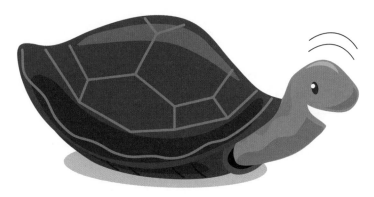

Where do you find a turtle with no legs?

—	—	—	—	—	—	—	—
36	60	72	16	72	24	72	16

—	—	—	—	—	—	—	—	—	—
7	45	25	48	25	18	60	40	30	.

Gridlock

WRITE numbers so that the product of the rows and columns is correct.

HINT: Use only the numbers 1 through 10.

Example:

	3	5
4	12	20
8	24	40

$3 \times 4 = 12$

$3 \times 8 = 24$

$5 \times 4 = 20$

$5 \times 8 = 40$

	4	7
	8	14

	5	6
	15	18

	18	63
	20	70

	10	16
	30	48

	21	56
	27	72

	35	42
	45	54

Pipe Down

WRITE the missing number. Then FOLLOW the pipe, and WRITE the same number in the next problem.

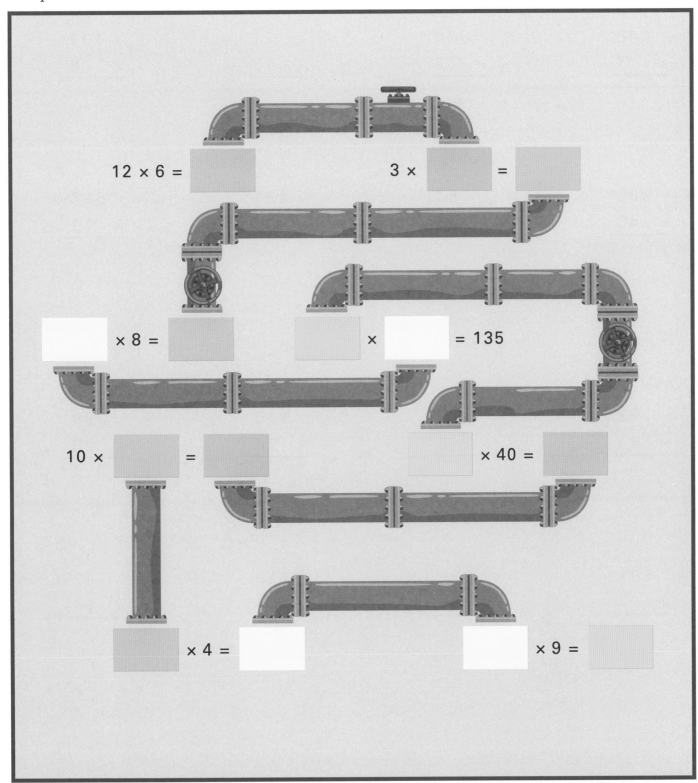

12 × 6 =

3 × ___ =

___ × 8 =

___ × ___ = 135

10 × ___ =

___ × 40 =

___ × 4 =

___ × 9 =

Criss Cross

SOLVE the multiplication problems, and WRITE the products in the puzzle.

ACROSS

1.
```
  148
×   7
```

4.
```
  824
×  68
```

5.
```
   21
×  13
```

7.
```
  401
×   8
```

9.
```
  335
×  43
```

10.
```
   64
×  45
```

11.
```
  491
×  52
```

12.
```
  528
×  71
```

DOWN

1.
```
   53
×  24
```

2.
```
  137
×   5
```

3.
```
  120
×  34
```

6.
```
  289
×  26
```

7.
```
  501
×   7
```

8.
```
  896
×  93
```

9.
```
  118
×  14
```

10.
```
   42
×  54
```

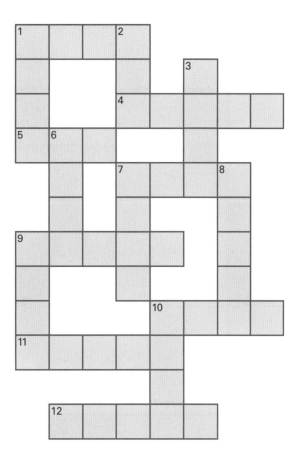

Super Square

WRITE numbers in the empty squares to finish all of the multiplication problems.

13	×	11	=	
×		×		×
6	×		=	
=		=		=
	×	154	=	

Code Breaker

SOLVE each problem. WRITE the letter that matches each quotient to solve the riddle.

1	2	3	4	5	6
9)63	7)56	3)30	12)12	4)16	9)18
C	O	H	A	T	E

7	8	9	10	11	12
9)45	2)22	8)24	3)36	5)30	8)72
G	F	U	I	L	S

How did the frog make the baseball team?

___ ___
10   2

___ ___ ___ ___ ___ ___
7   1   3   5   10   4

___   ___ ___ ___
1   6   8   4

___ ___   ___ ___ ___ ___ ___ .
8   11   11   6   12   2   9

Number Factory

WRITE the numbers that will come out of each machine.

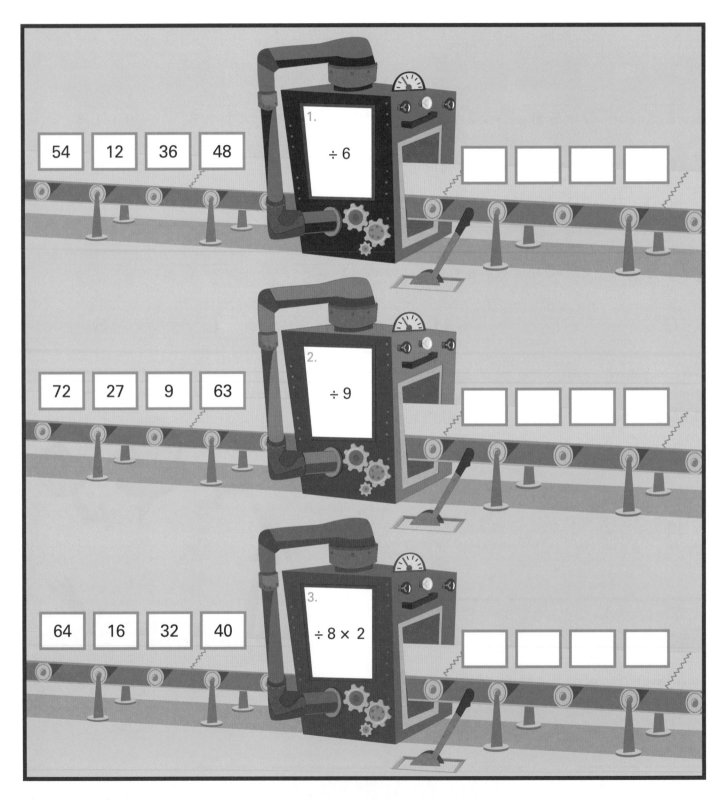

Pipe Down

WRITE the missing number. Then FOLLOW the pipe, and WRITE the same number in the next problem.

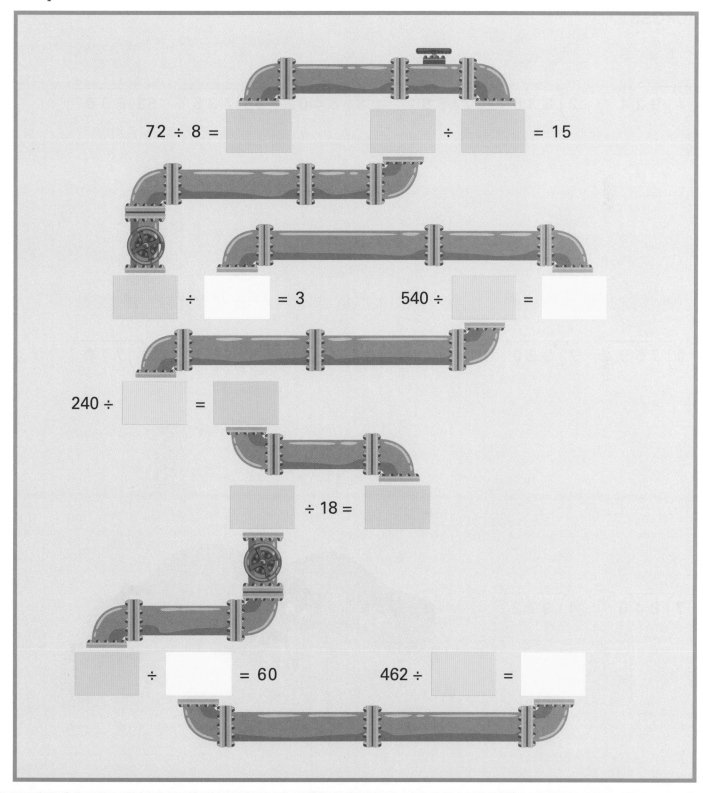

$72 \div 8 =$ ☐   ☐ $\div$ ☐ $= 15$

☐ $\div$ ☐ $= 3$ $540 \div$ ☐ $=$ ☐

$240 \div$ ☐ $=$ ☐

☐ $\div 18 =$ ☐

☐ $\div$ ☐ $= 60$ $462 \div$ ☐ $=$ ☐

Criss Cross

SOLVE the division problems, and WRITE the quotients in the puzzle.

ACROSS

1	4	7	8	9	11

$7\overline{)924}$ $\quad$ $2\overline{)836}$ $\quad$ $2\overline{)682}$ $\quad$ $8\overline{)840}$ $\quad$ $35\overline{)735}$ $\quad$ $58\overline{)696}$

13	14	15	16	19	21

$3\overline{)759}$ $\quad$ $2\overline{)920}$ $\quad$ $17\overline{)510}$ $\quad$ $28\overline{)812}$ $\quad$ $3\overline{)873}$ $\quad$ $2\overline{)770}$

24	25

$7\overline{)840}$ $\quad$ $4\overline{)972}$

1	2	3		4	5	6
7				8		
9	10				11	12
13				14		
15				16		
		17		18		
19	20			21	22	23
24				25		

DOWN

1
$$42\overline{)546}$$

2
$$8\overline{)272}$$

3
$$3\overline{)630}$$

4
$$2\overline{)838}$$

5
$$46\overline{)460}$$

6
$$11\overline{)935}$$

9
$$4\overline{)892}$$

10
$$5\overline{)750}$$

11
$$6\overline{)972}$$

12
$$3\overline{)627}$$

17
$$2\overline{)620}$$

18
$$1\overline{)532}$$

19
$$31\overline{)651}$$

20
$$8\overline{)736}$$

22
$$11\overline{)924}$$

23
$$16\overline{)848}$$

Multidigit Division

Super Square

WRITE numbers in the empty squares to finish all of the division problems.

972	÷	36	=	
÷		÷		÷
54	÷		=	
=		=		=
	÷	6	=	

What's the Password?

WRITE the letters that form a fraction of each word. Then WRITE the letters in order to find the secret password.

1. The first $\frac{1}{3}$ of **SURVEY** _____

2. The first $\frac{1}{7}$ of **MISSING** _____

3. The first $\frac{2}{9}$ of **MESMERIZE** _____

4. The last $\frac{1}{6}$ of **WINTER** _____

5. The first $\frac{3}{7}$ of **VACCINE** _____

6. The middle $\frac{1}{5}$ of **GRAVY** _____

7. The first $\frac{1}{2}$ of **TINY** _____

8. The last $\frac{2}{7}$ of **HEXAGON** _____

Password:

_____ _____ _____ _____ _____ _____

_____ _____ _____ _____ _____ _____

Recognizing Fractions & Decimals

Picking Pairs

DRAW a line to connect each decimal with the correct picture.

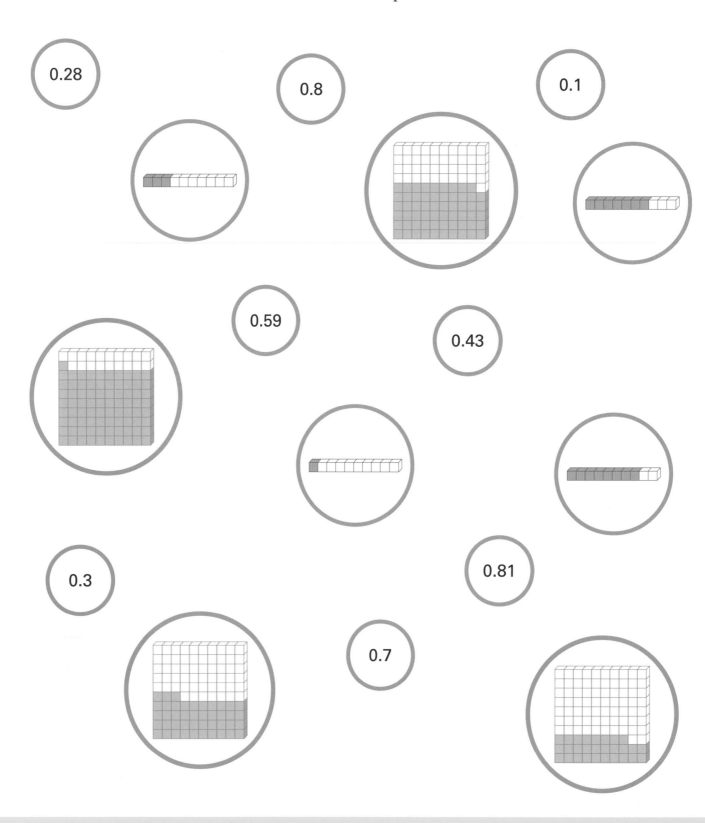

High Card

Use the cards from page 199. READ the rules. PLAY the game!

Rules: Two players
1. Decide if you want to play with fractions or decimals, and face the selected side down.
2. Deal all of the cards so both players have an equal stack of cards.
3. Both players flip a card over at the same time.
4. Whoever has the card with the biggest fraction or decimal gets to keep the cards.

The player with the most cards at the end wins!

Examples:

| $\dfrac{5}{8}$ | is bigger than | $\dfrac{1}{6}$ |

| 0.73 | is bigger than | 0.4 |

$\dfrac{7}{8}$ is bigger!

Totally Tangled

Each circle is connected to another numbered circle. FIND the pairs of decimals, and COLOR the smaller decimal.

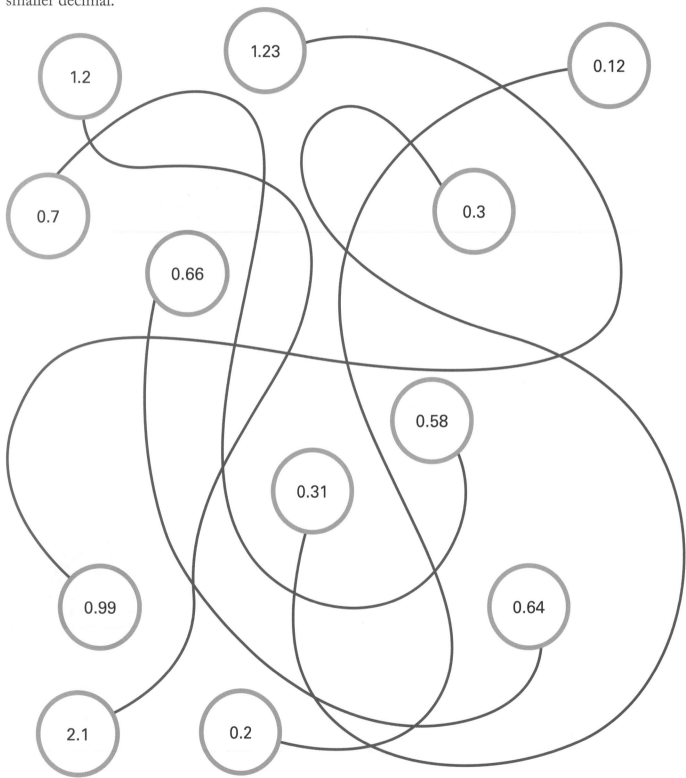

Code Breaker

SOLVE each problem. WRITE the letter that matches each sum to solve the riddle.

$\dfrac{1}{4} + \dfrac{2}{4} =$ [1] —— H	$\dfrac{1}{6} + \dfrac{4}{6} =$ [2] —— B	$\dfrac{2}{3} + \dfrac{1}{3} =$ [3] —— T
$\dfrac{1}{9} + \dfrac{4}{9} =$ [4] —— L	$\dfrac{3}{8} + \dfrac{4}{8} =$ [5] —— E	$\dfrac{1}{5} + \dfrac{1}{5} =$ [6] —— R
$\dfrac{1}{3} + \dfrac{1}{3} =$ [7] —— A	$\dfrac{3}{7} + \dfrac{2}{7} =$ [8] —— I	$\dfrac{2}{8} + \dfrac{3}{8} =$ [9] —— Y

Which building has the most stories?

___ ___ ___
$\dfrac{3}{3}$ $\dfrac{3}{4}$ $\dfrac{7}{8}$

___ ___ ___ ___ ___ ___ ___ .
$\dfrac{5}{9}$ $\dfrac{5}{7}$ $\dfrac{5}{6}$ $\dfrac{2}{5}$ $\dfrac{2}{3}$ $\dfrac{2}{5}$ $\dfrac{5}{8}$

Number Factory

WRITE the fractions that will come out of each machine.

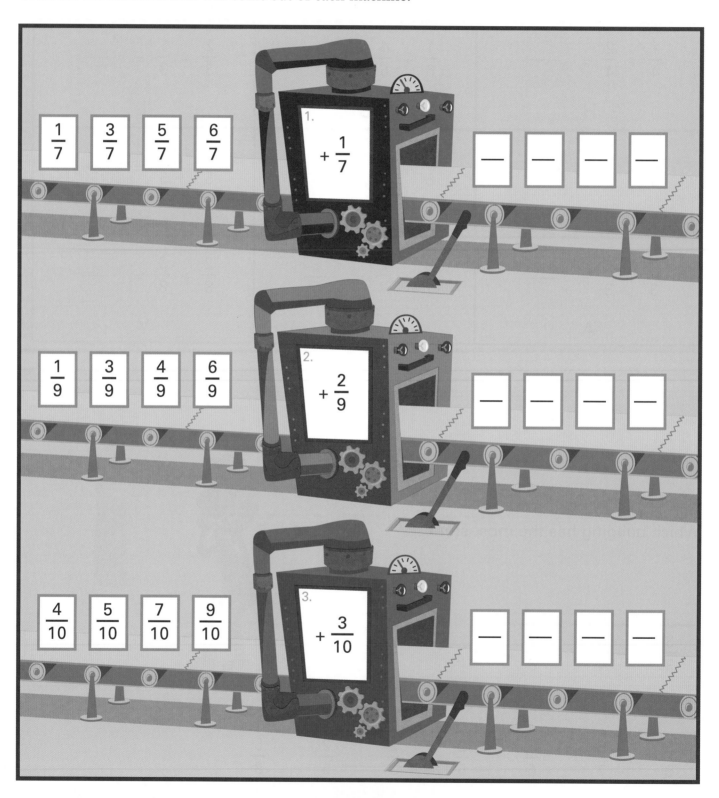

Code Breaker

SOLVE each problem. WRITE the letter that matches each difference to solve the riddle.

$\frac{3}{5} - \frac{1}{5} =$ ___ [1] E	$\frac{9}{12} - \frac{2}{12} =$ ___ [2] T	$\frac{7}{8} - \frac{4}{8} =$ ___ [3] U	$\frac{3}{3} - \frac{2}{3} =$ ___ [4] R
$\frac{4}{6} - \frac{1}{6} =$ ___ [5] S	$\frac{7}{7} - \frac{6}{7} =$ ___ [6] P	$\frac{3}{4} - \frac{2}{4} =$ ___ [7] H	$\frac{4}{5} - \frac{1}{5} =$ ___ [8] Y
$\frac{8}{9} - \frac{6}{9} =$ ___ [9] N	$\frac{6}{11} - \frac{4}{11} =$ ___ [10] I	$\frac{6}{6} - \frac{1}{6} =$ ___ [11] L	$\frac{8}{10} - \frac{5}{10} =$ ___ [12] O

How do snails talk to each other?

___ ___ ___ ___   ___ ___ ___
$\frac{7}{12}$ $\frac{1}{4}$ $\frac{2}{5}$ $\frac{3}{5}$ $\frac{3}{8}$ $\frac{3}{6}$ $\frac{2}{5}$

___ ___ ___ ___ ___   ___ ___ ___ ___ ___
$\frac{7}{12}$ $\frac{1}{4}$ $\frac{2}{5}$ $\frac{2}{11}$ $\frac{1}{3}$ $\frac{3}{6}$ $\frac{1}{4}$ $\frac{2}{5}$ $\frac{5}{6}$ $\frac{5}{6}$

___ ___ ___ ___ ___ ___.
$\frac{1}{7}$ $\frac{1}{4}$ $\frac{3}{10}$ $\frac{2}{9}$ $\frac{2}{5}$ $\frac{3}{6}$

Adding & Subtracting Fractions

Number Factory

WRITE the fractions that will come out of each machine.

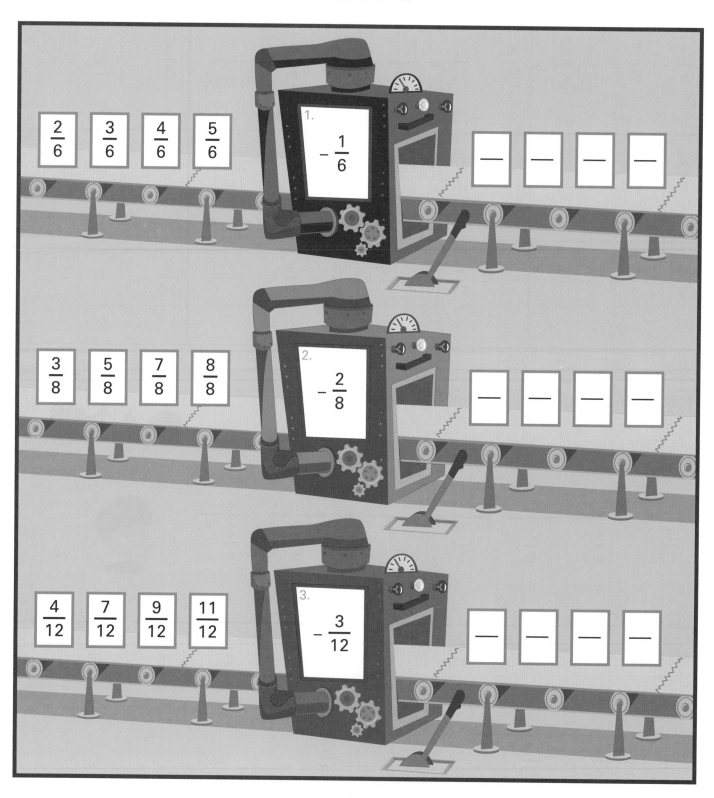

Code Breaker

SOLVE each problem. WRITE the letter that matches each sum or difference to solve the riddle.

3.5 + 6.2	1.4 + 2.1	2.38 + 1.43	4.92 + 3.55	3.82 + 4.2	5.6 + 4.59
1	2	3	4	5	6
I	T	E	A	N	L

8.6 − 2.5	9.9 − 4.3	7.05 − 2.62	10.51 − 8.67	12.43 − 9.5
7	8	9	10	11
W	O	M	G	B

What time is it when an
elephant sits on your table?

3.5	9.7	4.43	3.81		3.5	5.6		1.84	3.81	3.5

8.47		8.02	3.81	6.1		3.5	8.47	2.93	10.19	3.81

Adding & Subtracting Decimals

Number Factory

WRITE the numbers that will come out of each machine.

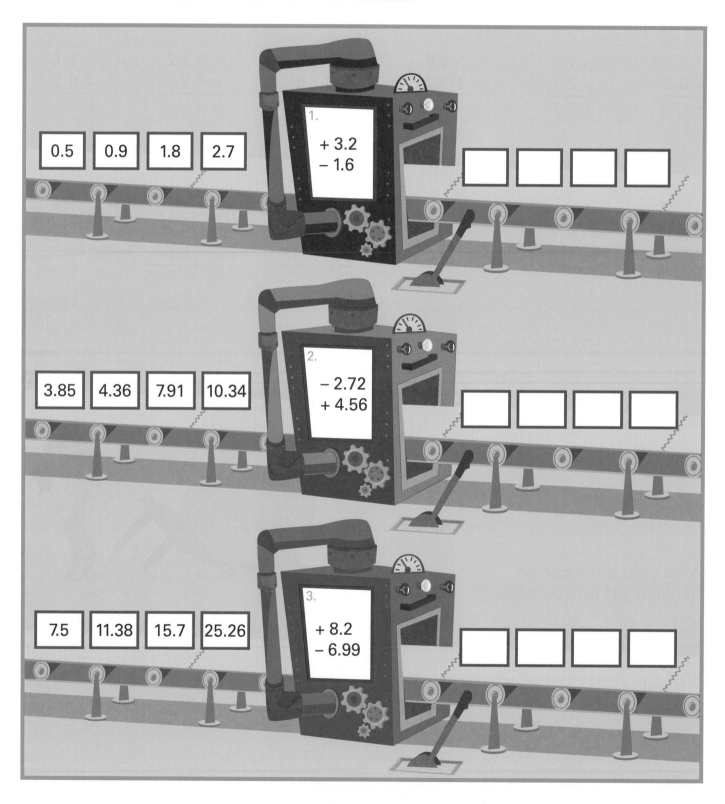

1. + 3.2 − 1.6

0.5   0.9   1.8   2.7

2. − 2.72 + 4.56

3.85   4.36   7.91   10.34

3. + 8.2 − 6.99

7.5   11.38   15.7   25.26

Pipe Down

WRITE the missing number. Then FOLLOW the pipe, and WRITE the same number in the next problem.

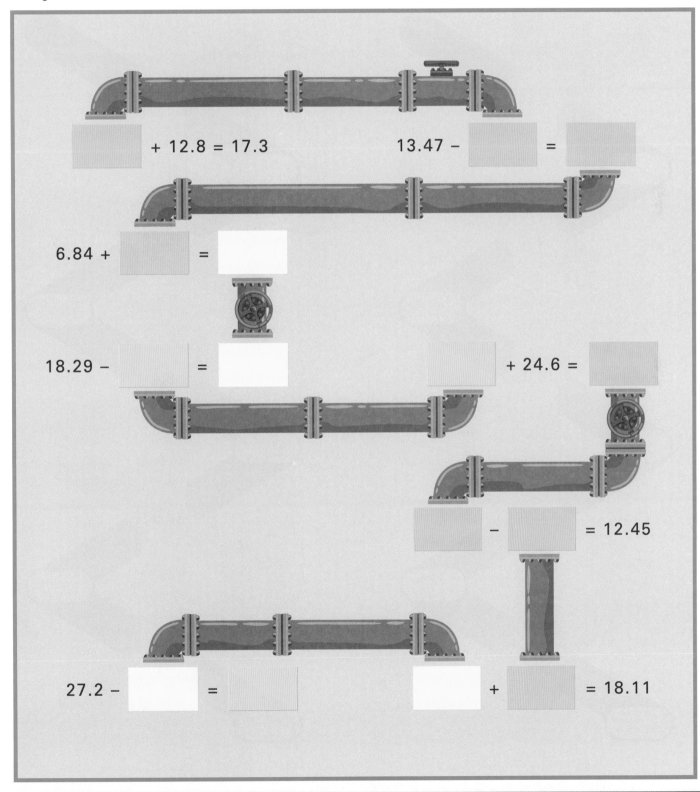

____ + 12.8 = 17.3

13.47 − ____ = ____

6.84 + ____ = ____

18.29 − ____ = ____

____ + 24.6 = ____

____ − ____ = 12.45

27.2 − ____ = ____

____ + ____ = 18.11

Crossing Paths

WRITE the missing numbers.

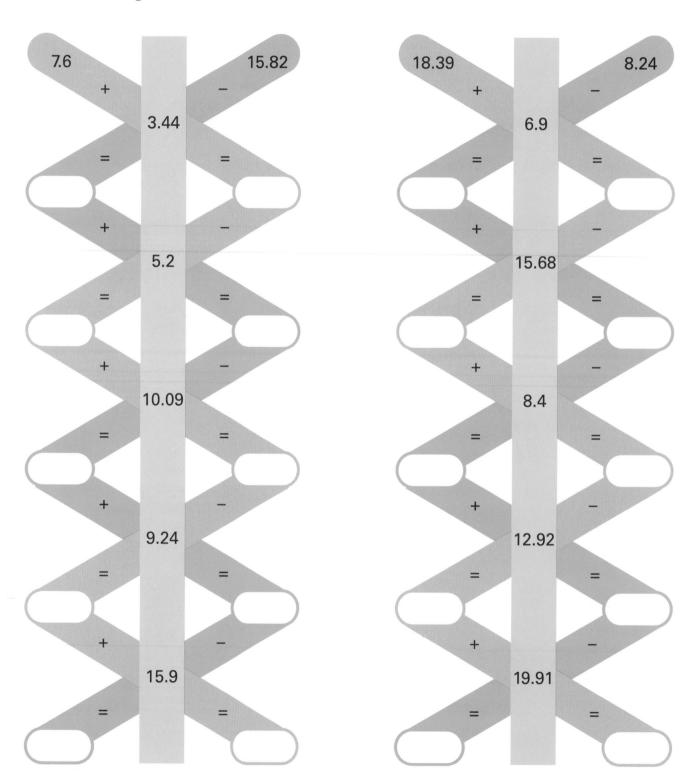

Code Ruler

WRITE the letter that matches each measurement to answer the riddle.

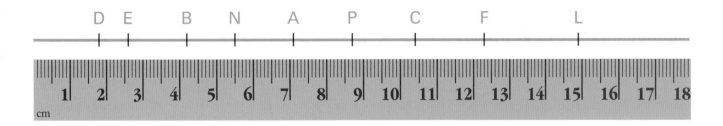

What runs around the yard without moving?

___ ___ ___ ___ ___ ___ .

7.1 cm   12.3 cm 2.6 cm 5.5 cm 10.4 cm 2.6 cm

Totally Tangled

FIND the measurements that are connected. COLOR the smaller measurement in each pair.

1 centimeter (cm) = 10 millimeters (mm)
1 meter (m) = 100 centimeters
1 kilometer (km) = 1,000 meters

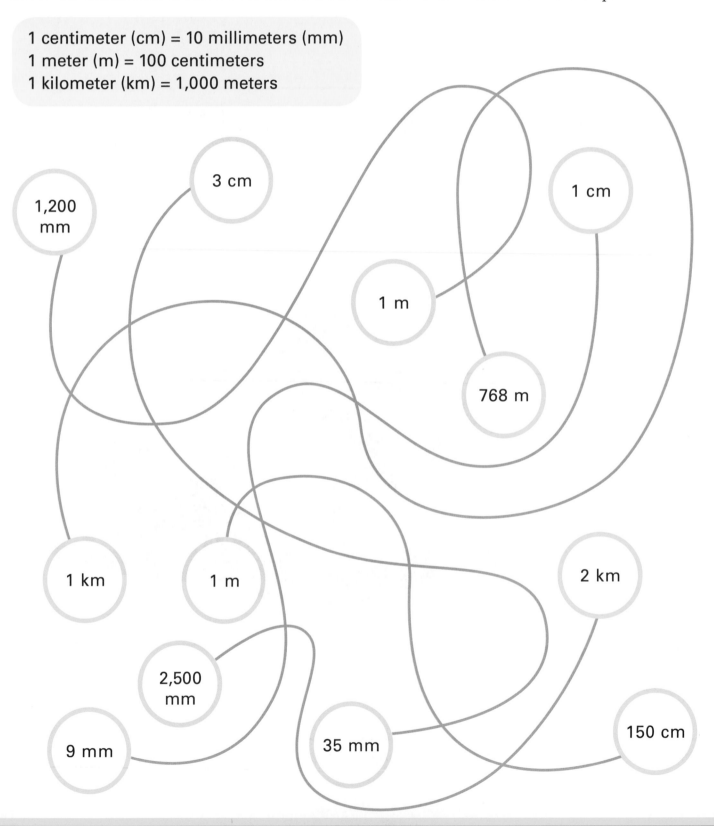

Code Ruler

WRITE the letter that matches each measurement to answer the riddle.

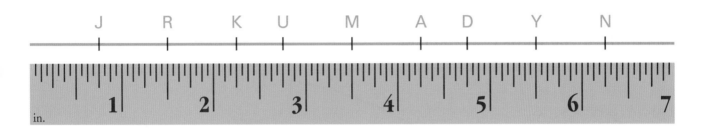

J   R   K   U   M   A   D   Y   N

in.   1   2   3   4   5   6   7

What do you call three feet of garbage?

_____   _____ _____ _____ _____ _____ _____ _____ _____.

$4\frac{1}{4}$ in. $\frac{3}{4}$ in. $2\frac{3}{4}$ in. $6\frac{1}{4}$ in. $2\frac{1}{4}$ in. $5\frac{1}{2}$ in. $4\frac{1}{4}$ in. $1\frac{1}{2}$ in. $4\frac{3}{4}$ in.

Length

Totally Tangled

FIND the measurements that are connected. COLOR the larger measurement in each pair.

1 foot (ft) = 12 inches (in.)
1 yard (yd) = 3 feet
1 mile (mi) = 1,760 yards or 5,280 feet

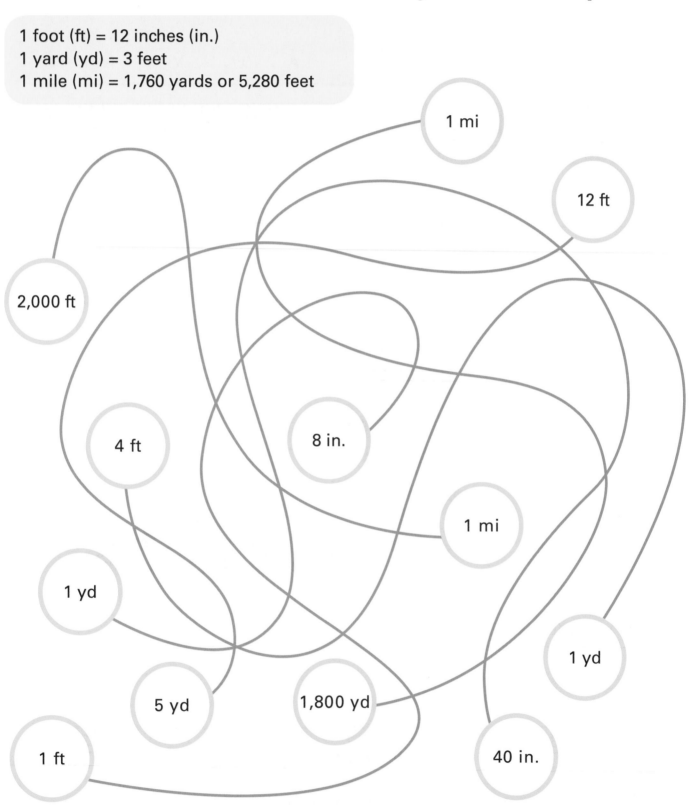

Puzzling Pentominoes

Perimeter is the distance around a two-dimensional shape. Use the pentomino pieces from page 201, and PLACE the pieces to completely fill each shape without overlapping any pieces. Then WRITE the perimeter of each shape. (Save the pentomino pieces to use again later in the workbook.)

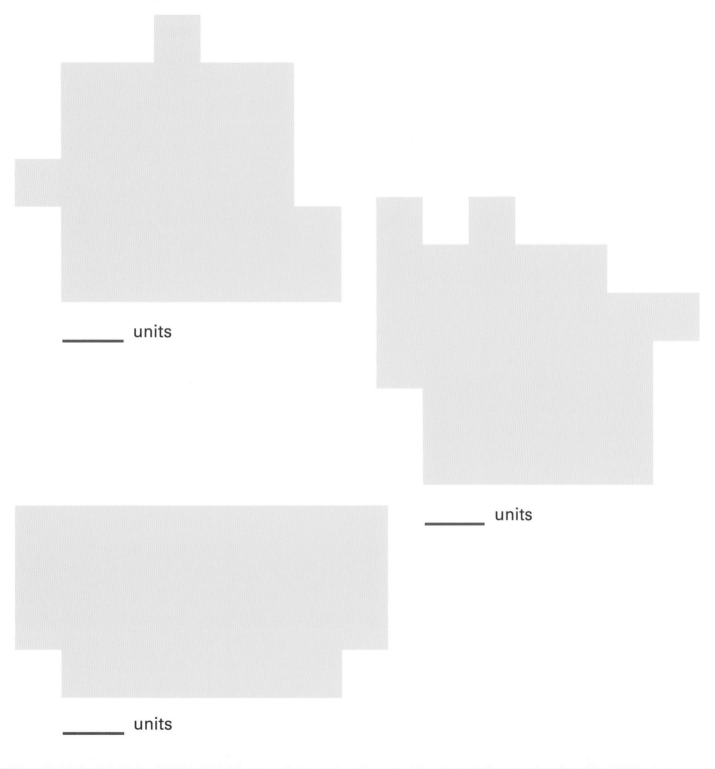

_____ units

_____ units

_____ units

Shape Creator

DRAW three different shapes that all have a perimeter of 12 units.

Using a centimeter ruler, DRAW two different shapes with a perimeter of 20 centimeters.

Puzzling Pentominoes

Area is the size of the surface of a shape, and it is measured in square units. Use the pentomino pieces from page 201, and PLACE the pieces to completely fill each shape without overlapping any pieces. Then WRITE the area of each shape.

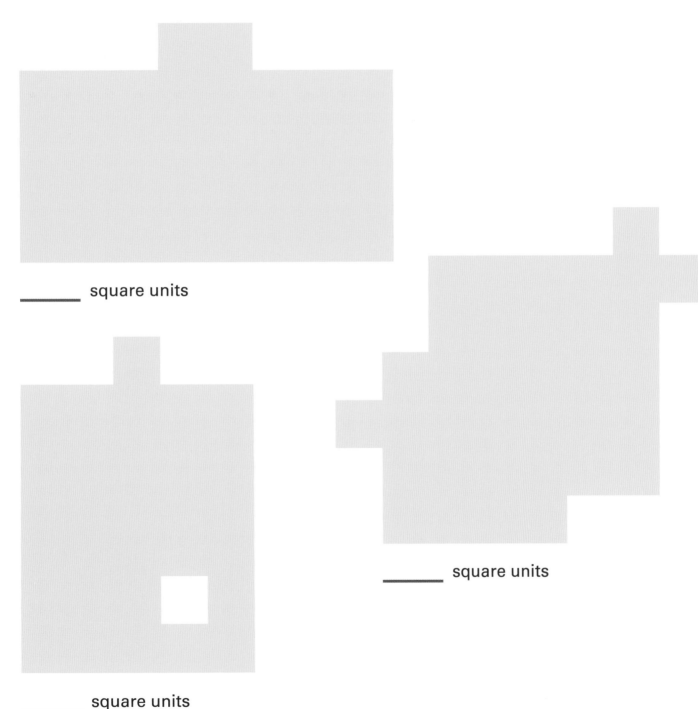

_____ square units

_____ square units

_____ square units

Shape Creator

DRAW three different shapes that all have an area of 10 square units.

Using a centimeter ruler, DRAW two different rectangles with an area of 24 square centimeters.

Code Breaker

SOLVE each problem. WRITE the letter that matches each equivalent measurement to solve the riddle.

1 gram (g) = 1,000 milligrams (mg)	1 kilogram (kg) = 1,000 grams

1 5 g = _____ mg	D	2 2,300 g = _____ kg	L
3 6 kg = _____ g	O	4 600 mg = _____ g	A
5 3,000 mg = _____ g	H	6 6.5 g = _____ mg	U
7 1.5 kg = _____ g	C	8 10,400 g = _____ kg	N
9 0.2 g = _____ mg	Y	10 1,000,000 mg = _____ kg	E

What can you add to a barrel to make it lighter?

200	6,000	6,500		1,500	0.6	10.4		0.6	5,000	5,000

0.6		3	6,000	2.3	1	.

Totally Tangled

FIND the measurements that are connected. COLOR the smaller measurement in each pair.

1 gram (g) = 1,000 milligrams (mg)   1 kilogram (kg) = 1,000 grams

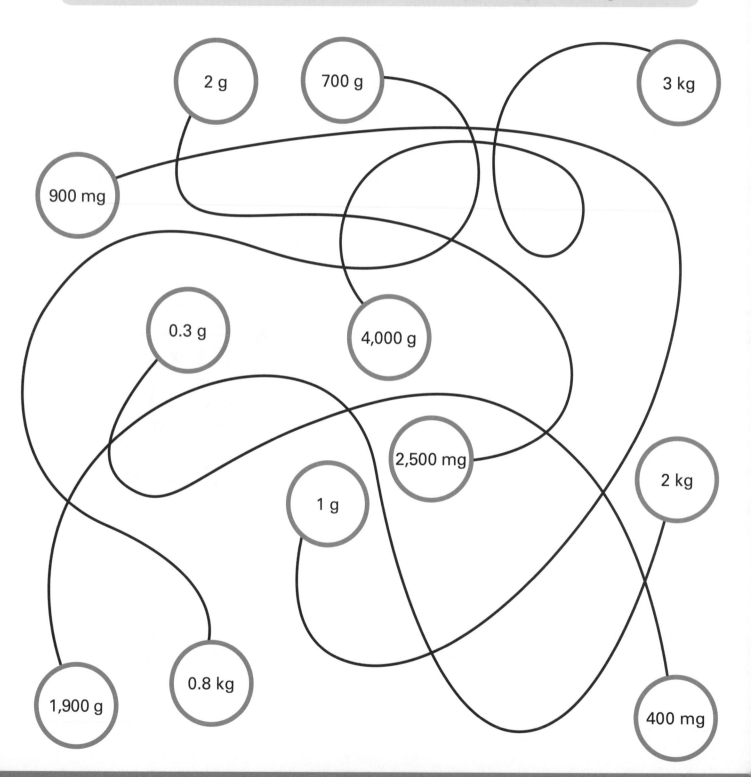

Code Breaker

SOLVE each problem. Use a fraction where necessary. WRITE the letter that matches each equivalent measurement to solve the riddle.

1 pound (lb) = 16 ounces (oz)	1 ton (T) = 2,000 pounds

1 4,000 lb = _____ T	T	2 24 oz = _____ lb	I
3 2 lb = _____ oz	W	4 $\frac{1}{4}$ T = _____ lb	N
5 3T = _____ lb	Y	6 5,000 lb = _____ T	B
7 32,000 oz = _____ T	O	8 $\frac{3}{4}$ lb = _____ oz	G
9 $\frac{1}{2}$ lb = _____ oz	H	10 $2\frac{3}{4}$ T = _____ lb	E

What weighs more, a ton of rocks or a ton of leaves?

___ ___ ___ ___   ___ ___ ___ ___
2   8   5,500 6,000 $2\frac{1}{2}$ 1   2   8

___ ___ ___ ___ ___
32 5,500 $1\frac{1}{2}$ 12   8

___ ___ ___   ___ ___ ___ .
1   500 5,500   2   1   500

Totally Tangled

FIND the measurements that are connected. COLOR the larger measurement in each pair.

1 pound (lb) = 16 ounces (oz)   1 ton (T) = 2,000 pounds

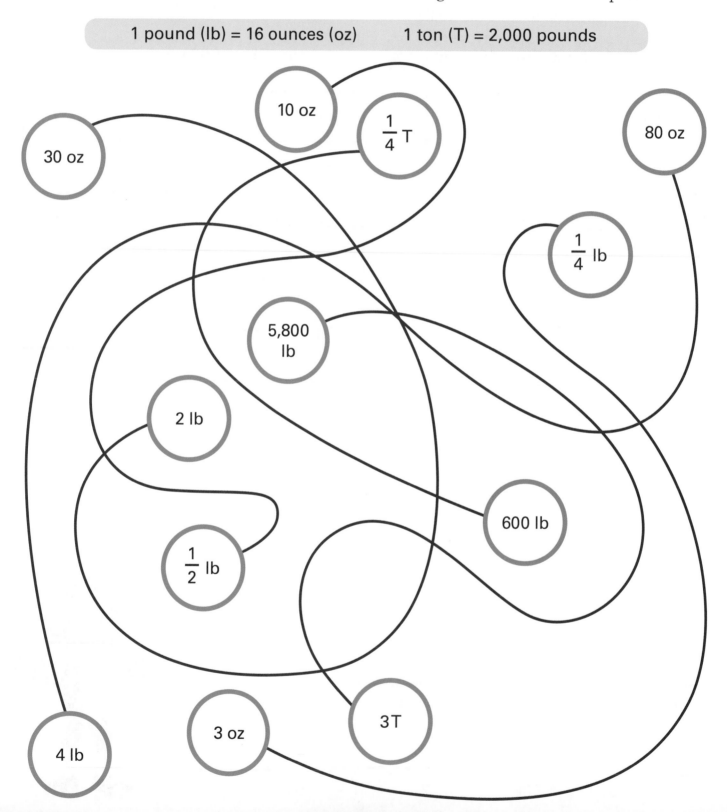

10 oz

$\frac{1}{4}$ T

30 oz

80 oz

$\frac{1}{4}$ lb

5,800 lb

2 lb

600 lb

$\frac{1}{2}$ lb

4 lb

3 oz

3 T

Who Am I?

READ the clues, and CIRCLE the mystery shape.

HINT: Cross out any shape that does not match the clues.

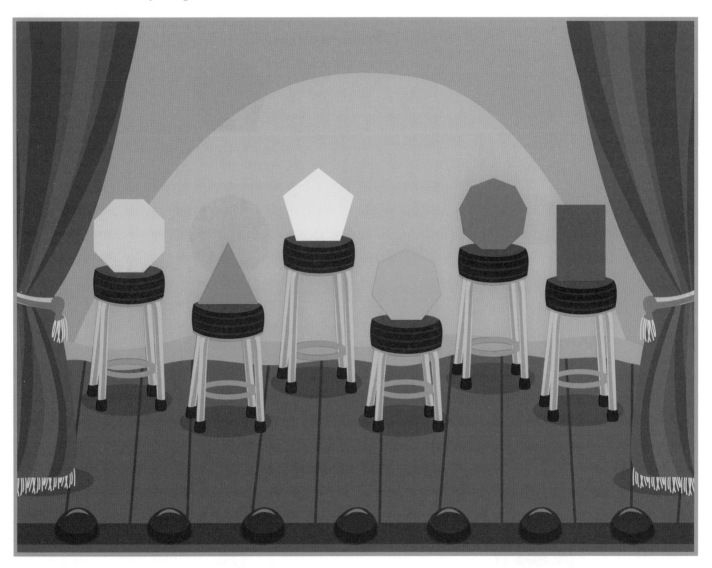

I have fewer than nine sides.

I have no acute angles.

I have more than five sides.

I have seven vertices.

Who am I?

Criss Cross

IDENTIFY each shape, and WRITE the shape names in the puzzle.

ACROSS

2.

3.

6.

7.

DOWN

1.

2.

4.

5.

Fold the Square

Origami is the Japanese art of paper folding, and it often starts with just one simple square. CUT OUT a square piece of paper that is at least six inches by six inches. FOLLOW the steps to make your own paper box.

HINT: Be sure to get a nice crease with each fold.

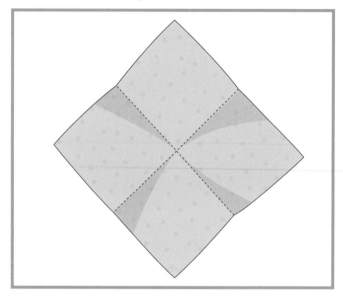

1. Fold the square in half both ways to find a center point.

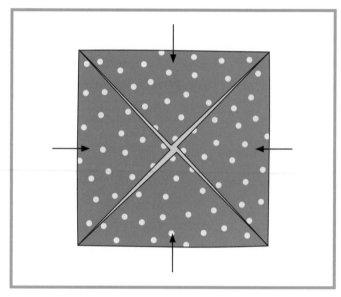

2. Fold the corners into the center, forming a square made from four triangles.

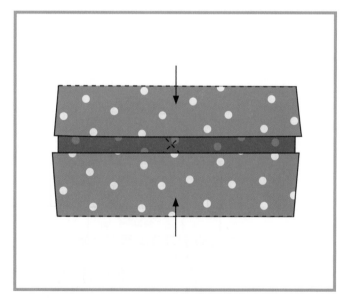

3. Fold two opposite sides into the center.

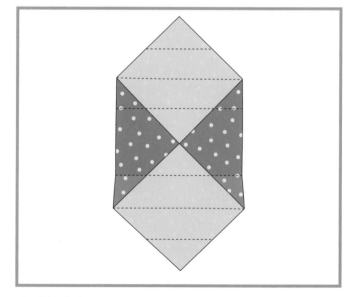

4. Unfold the same two sides until the points are pointing out.

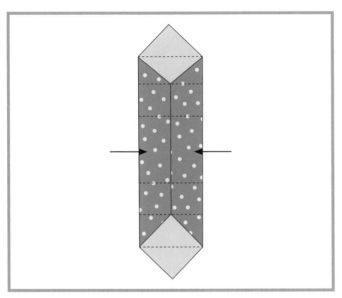

5. Now fold the other two sides into the center.

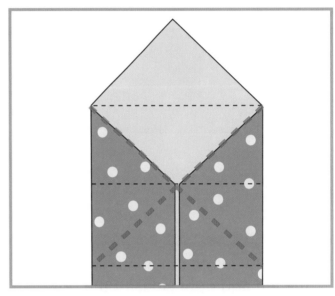

6a. Fold toward you along the angled (red dotted) lines to make creases in the paper.

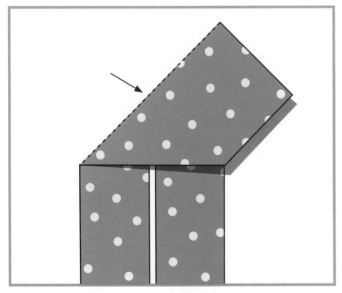

6b. Fold the top part to the right. Then unfold and fold to the left. Creating these creases will make the box easier to fold.

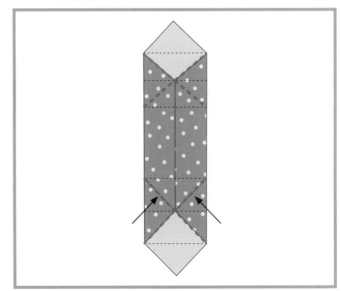

6c. Repeat this on both ends until you've made four creases (red dotted lines).

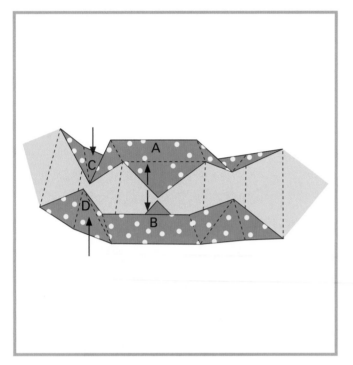

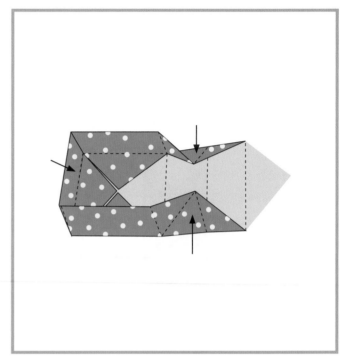

7. Partially unfold the paper to create the left and right sides of the box. Lift up at A and B while pushing in at C and D.

8. Follow the creases of the paper and tuck one end of the long side into the bottom of the box. Repeat on the other side.

Your box is finished and you're ready to store your treats and treasures.

Try following these steps with a larger piece of paper. You can also make a box with a lid if you use two different squares, one slightly larger than the other.

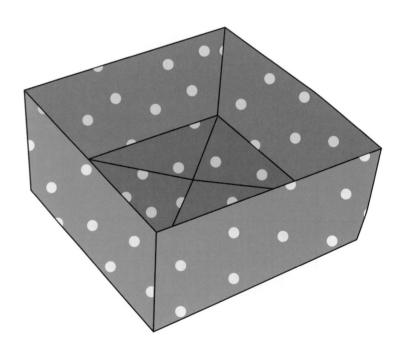

Who Am I?

READ the clues, and CIRCLE the mystery shape.

HINT: Cross out any shape that does not match the clues.

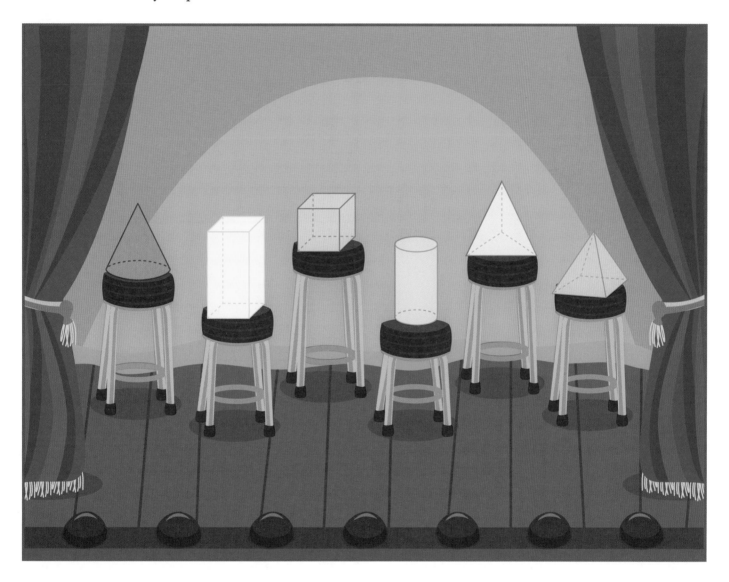

You'll find no round face on me.

I have more than six edges.

I have at least two square faces.

I have four rectangular faces.

Who am I?

Criss Cross

IDENTIFY each shape, and WRITE the shape names in the puzzle.

ACROSS

3.

4.

5.

DOWN

1.

2.

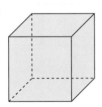

4.

Shape Scavenging

Use these scorecards, and go on a shape scavenger hunt. READ the rules. PLAY the game!

Rules: Two players or teams
1. Pick a location and a time limit for your scavenger hunt. For example, your scavenger hunt can be inside the house for 20 minutes, or each player can pick a different room.
2. When you find something that has the same shape as the shapes on the scorecards, write its name. Shapes that are harder to find earn more points.
3. At the end of the scavenger hunt, add up your points.

The player or team with the most points wins!

Rectangular prism: 5 points	Cylinder: 8 points	Sphere: 10 points
Cube: 12 points	Cone: 15 points	Square pyramid: 20 points

PLAYER 1

	Items Found	Points
	Total Points	

PLAYER 2

	Items Found	Points
	Total Points	

Shape Builders

CUT OUT each shape on the opposite page. FOLD on the dotted lines, and GLUE the tabs to construct each solid shape. Then WRITE the answers to the questions.

1. What is the name of the blue shape? _____

2. What is the name of the yellow shape? _____

3. Which shape is taller? _____

4. How many faces does the blue shape have? _____

5. How many faces does the yellow shape have? _____

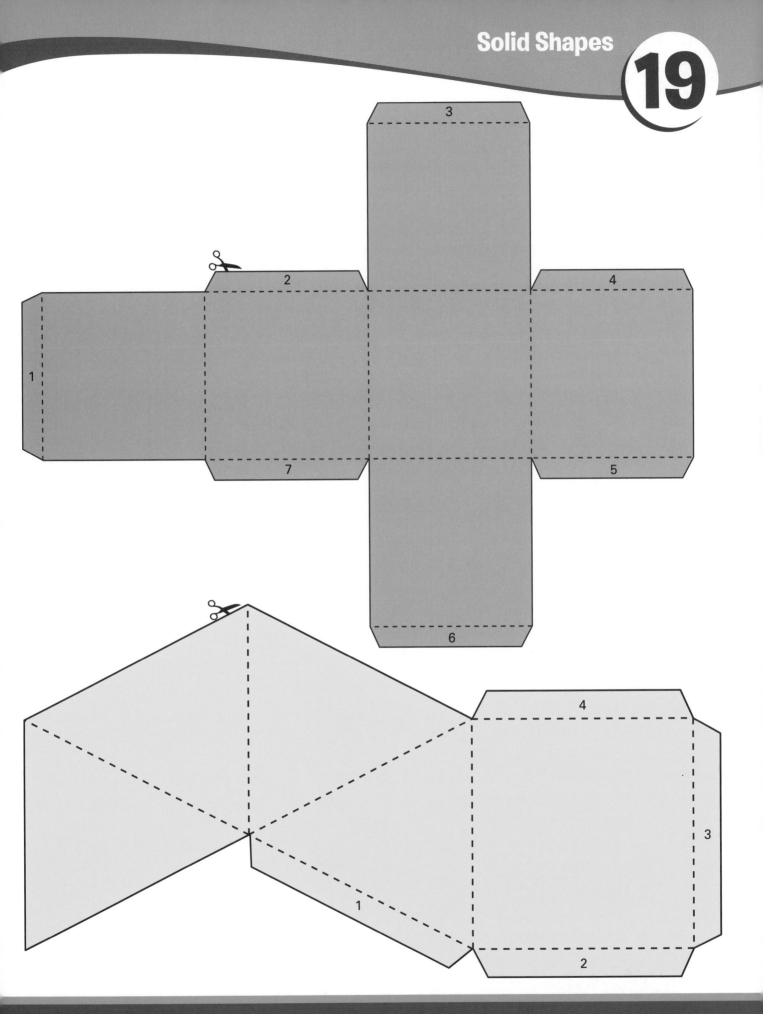

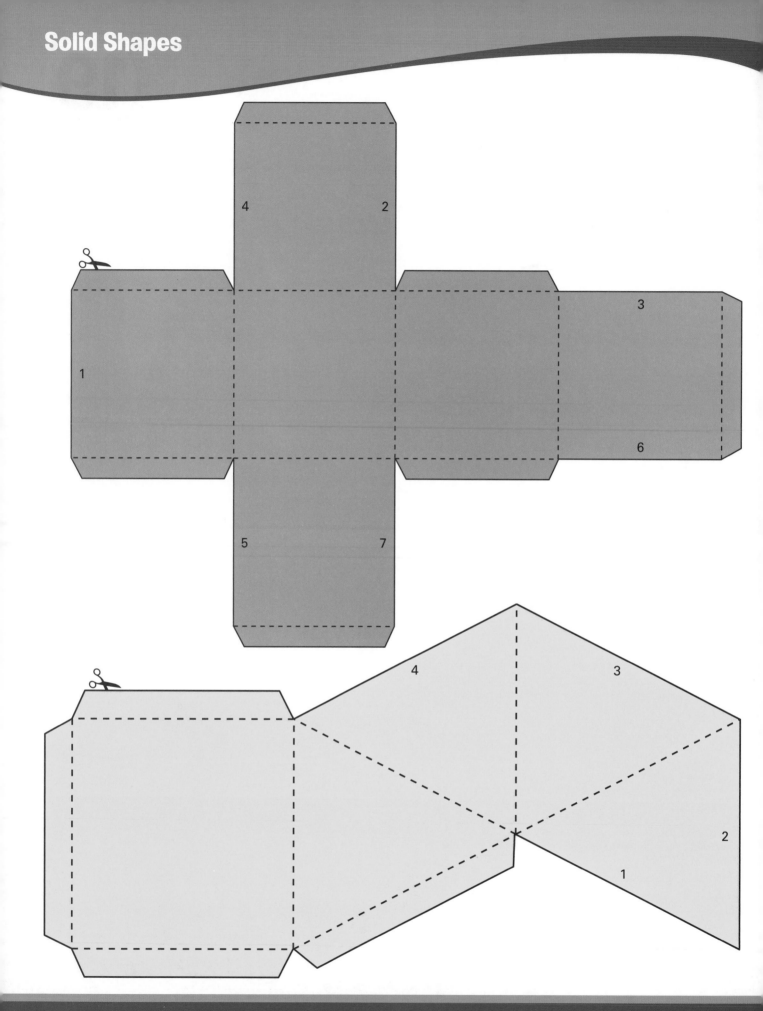

Tricky Tangrams

Use the tangram pieces from page 203, and PLACE the pieces to completely fill each shape without overlapping any pieces. (Save the tangram pieces to use again.)

HINT: Try placing the biggest pieces first.

Tricky Tangrams

Use the tangram pieces from page 203, and PLACE the pieces to completely fill each shape without overlapping any pieces.

HINT: Try placing the biggest pieces first.

Incredible Illusions

A **tessellation** is a repeating pattern of shapes that has no gaps or overlapping shapes. COLOR the rest of the tessellation. Do the rows of shapes look straight or bent?

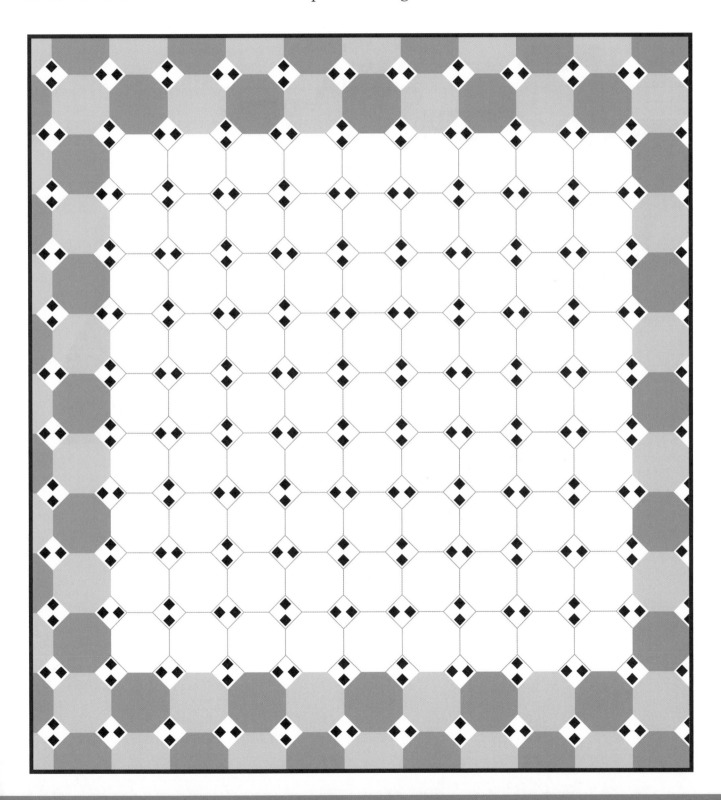

Shape Shifters

Use the pattern block pieces from page 205, and PLACE the pieces to finish the tessellation without overlapping any pieces.

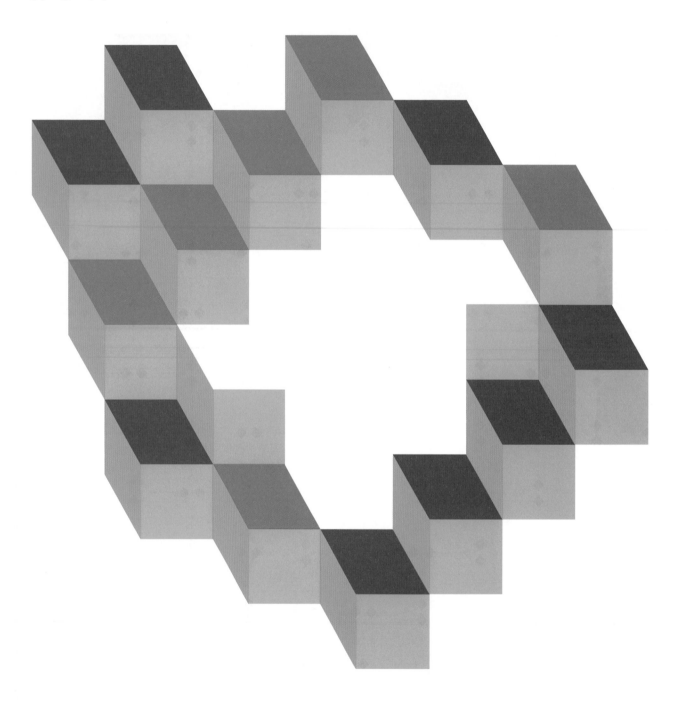

T-Shirt Shop

READ the paragraph, and WRITE the answer.

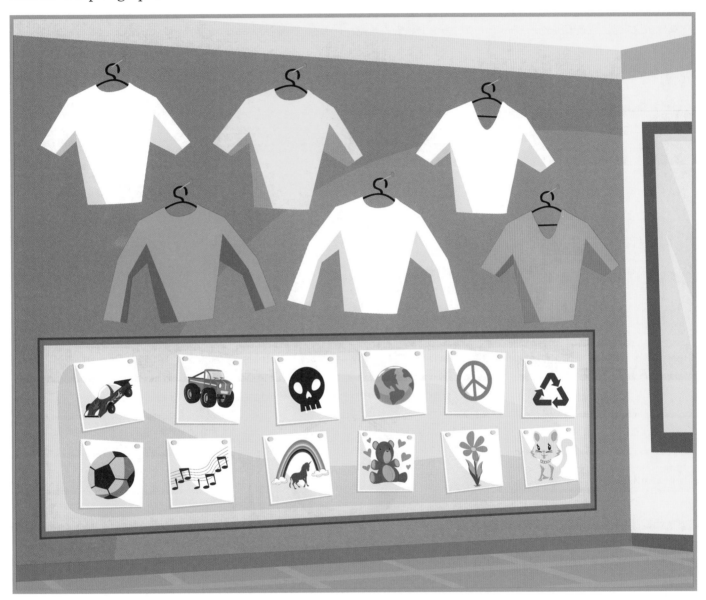

A T-shirt shop can put any design on the T-shirt of your choice. There are 6 different T-shirts and 12 different designs, and you can choose to have your name put on the back or not. How many different T-shirts can you make?

_____ T-shirts

All You Can Eat

READ the paragraph, and WRITE the answer.

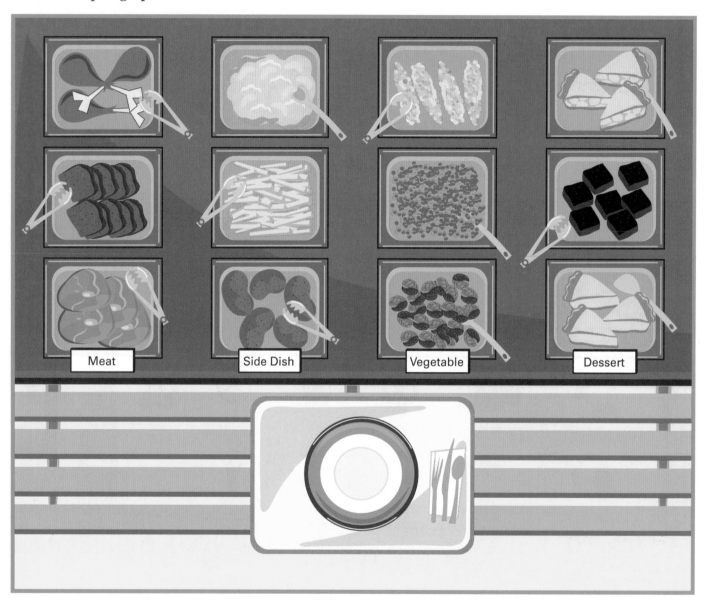

Each time you go to the buffet, your plate should have a choice of one meat, one side dish, one vegetable, and one dessert. How many times can you visit the buffet and get a different plate of food?

_____ times

Bus Ride

READ the clues, and CIRCLE the answer.

The Gallagher sisters always sit together.
Andrew sits next to Alyssa and behind Bill.
Stella likes to sit in back.
Bill always takes the window seat next to Nolan.
Kayley sits in front of Becky.
Dan sits in the aisle seat next to Ella.

Where is Dan in this picture?

In the Neighborhood

WRITE the name of each family on the correct mailbox.

The Green family chose their house for its color.

The Park family is always complaining about the noise coming from the Taguchi house next door.

The Simpsons live across the street from the Green family.

The Taguchis don't like looking out their front window at the Links' lawn flamingoes.

The Meyers live between the Links and the Simpsons.

Colorful Campground

Each tent is a different color. READ the clues, and COLOR each tent red, blue, yellow, green, orange, or purple.

The blue tent is west of the road.

The orange tent is below the lake.

The purple tent is north of the green tent.

The tent farthest south is not orange or purple.

The tent closest to the lake is green.

The red tent has a view of the entire campground.

Secret Location

FIND the points on the map, and WRITE the name of the country at those coordinates. Then UNSCRAMBLE the letters in red to find the secret location on the map.

HINT: Find the first number along the bottom, and the second number along the side. Then find the point where the two lines meet.

1. | 2, 8

2. | 3, 2

3. | 8, 3

4. | 7, 11

5. | 13, 8

6. | 5, 4

7. | 7, 7

Secret location:

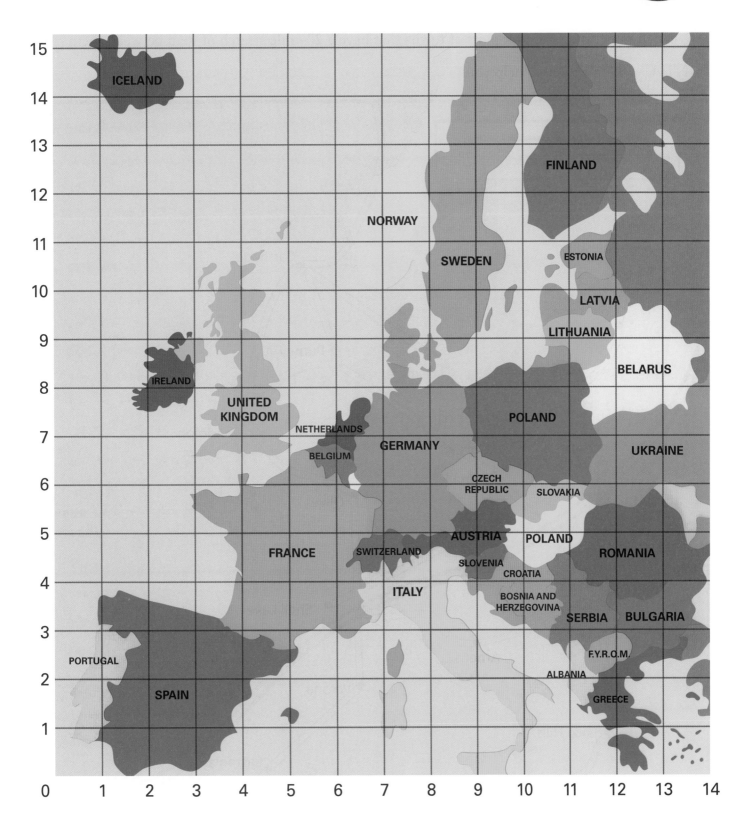

Distant Places

DRAW lines between the four pairs of towns that have a 20-mile stretch of road between them.

HINT: Use the map key to help you.

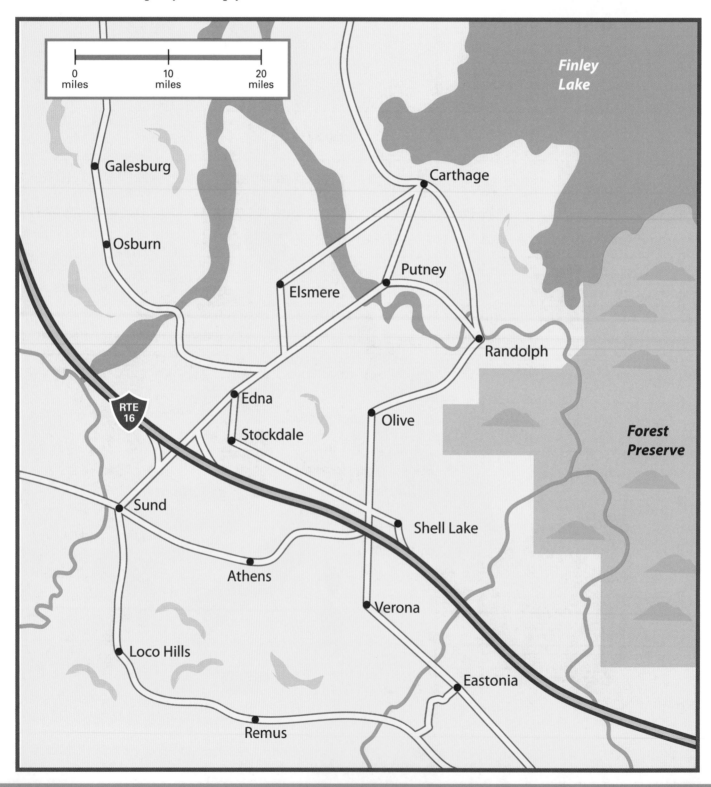

Flip a Coin

Probability is used to describe the chance of something happening. It can be represented by a number from 0 to 1.

Example: The probability that you will grow to be 30 feet tall is 0.

The probability that the sun will rise tomorrow morning is 1.

The probability of getting heads on a coin flip is $\frac{1}{2}$.

To see how probability works, try playing this game. FLIP a coin three times, and WRITE whether you flip heads or tails. SCORE 20 points for turns where you flip either three heads or three tails. SCORE 8 points for turns where you flip heads, heads, tails or tails, tails, heads. SCORE 5 points for any other coin combination. REPEAT this three more times. Then ANSWER the questions.

1	2	3	Score

1	2	3	Score

1	2	3	Score

1	2	3	Score

Total Score: _____

1. What is the chance of scoring 80 points in this game?
    impossible   unlikely   likely   certain

2. What is the chance of scoring 15 points in this game?
    impossible   unlikely   likely   certain

3. What is the chance of scoring at least 20 points in this game?
    impossible   unlikely   likely   certain

Cat's out of the Bag

CUT OUT the pieces from the opposite page, and PUT them in a bag. READ the rules. PLAY the game! Then ANSWER the questions.

HINT: Think about the fraction of each animal to the total number of cards.

Rules: Two players
1. Take turns picking cards out of the bag.
2. Keep picking until all three cats have been found.

The player with the most cats wins!

There are 3 cats, 9 dogs, and 12 mice.

1. What is the probability that you will pull a cat out of the bag on the first turn?

    0     $\frac{1}{8}$ $\frac{1}{4}$ $\frac{1}{2}$ 1

2. What is the probability that you will pull a mouse out of the bag on the first turn?

    0     $\frac{1}{8}$ $\frac{1}{4}$ $\frac{1}{2}$ 1

3. How likely is it that the game will be a tie?

    impossible   unlikely   likely   certain

4. How likely is it that the game will be over after three turns?

    impossible   unlikely   likely   certain

5. How likely is it that three cats will be pulled out of the bag before the game ends?

    impossible   unlikely   likely   certain

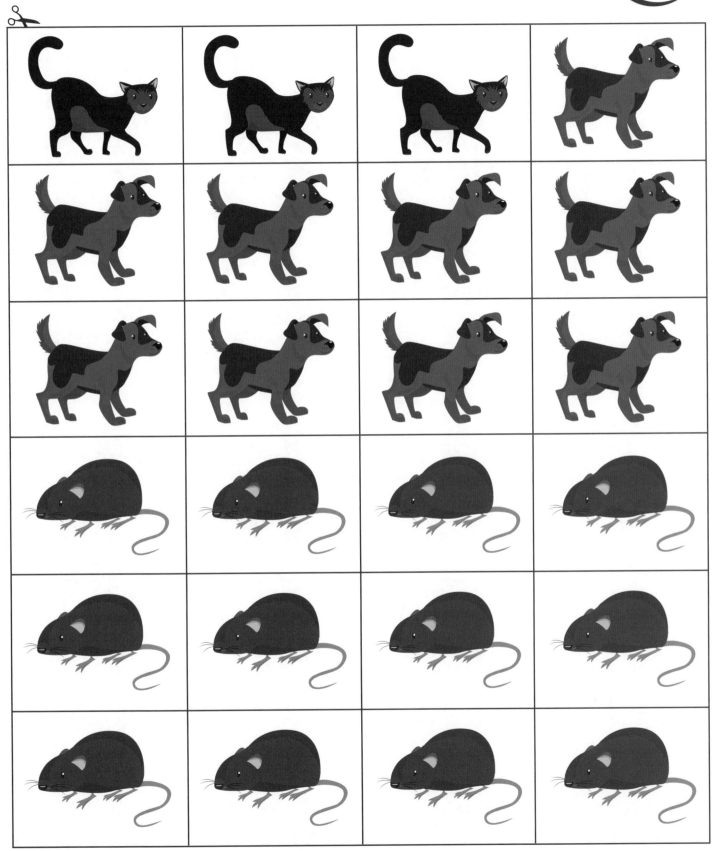

Time Twins

In one day, how many times does a clock have times where all of the digits are the same?

HINT: Don't forget a.m. and p.m.

_____ times

Rail Race

READ the clues. Then WRITE the number of the train each person took, and CIRCLE the person who got to Washington DC first.

My train departed at 3:50 p.m., exactly 8 minutes late.

Train _____
1

I live near Boston. I left the house at 11:00, and it takes me about 45 minutes to get to the train station.

Train _____
2

My mom and I missed the 8:24 train in Providence, so we caught the next one.

Train _____
3

I always take the train that gets me from Wilmington to Washington in the shortest amount of time.

Train _____
4

TRAIN SCHEDULE

	33	75	19	41	68	92
Boston, MA	7:42 a.m.	9:35 a.m.	10:40 a.m.	11:25 a.m.	12:31 p.m.	1:47 p.m.
Providence, RI	8:24 a.m.	10:16 a.m.	11:22 a.m.	12:05 p.m.	1:11 p.m.	2:26 p.m.
New Haven, CT	10:18 a.m.	12:11 p.m.	1:20 p.m.	2:01 p.m.	3:10 p.m.	4:25 p.m.
New York, NY	11:58 a.m.	1:50 p.m.	2:59 p.m.	3:42 p.m.	4:49 p.m.	6:07 p.m.
Trenton, NJ	1:01 p.m.	2:53 p.m.	4:02 p.m.	4:47 p.m.	5:53 p.m.	7:10 p.m.
Wilmington, DE	2:06 p.m.	3:54 p.m.	5:10 p.m.	5:50 p.m.	7:03 p.m.	8:18 p.m.
Baltimore, MD	3:14 p.m.	5:02 p.m.	6:14 p.m.	6:58 p.m.	8:09 p.m.	9:24 p.m.
Washington DC	4:30 p.m.	6:13 p.m.	7:21 p.m.	8:10 p.m.	9:19 p.m.	10:38 p.m.

Holding Hands

In one day, how many times do the hour and minute hands cross each other on a clock? WRITE the answer.

HINT: After 12:00, the first time that the clock hands cross each other is around 1:06. Think about what times the clock hands cross, and draw them on the clock to help you count. Try using a watch if you get stuck.

_____ times

Pocket Change

DRAW three straight lines to create six different money sets of equal value.

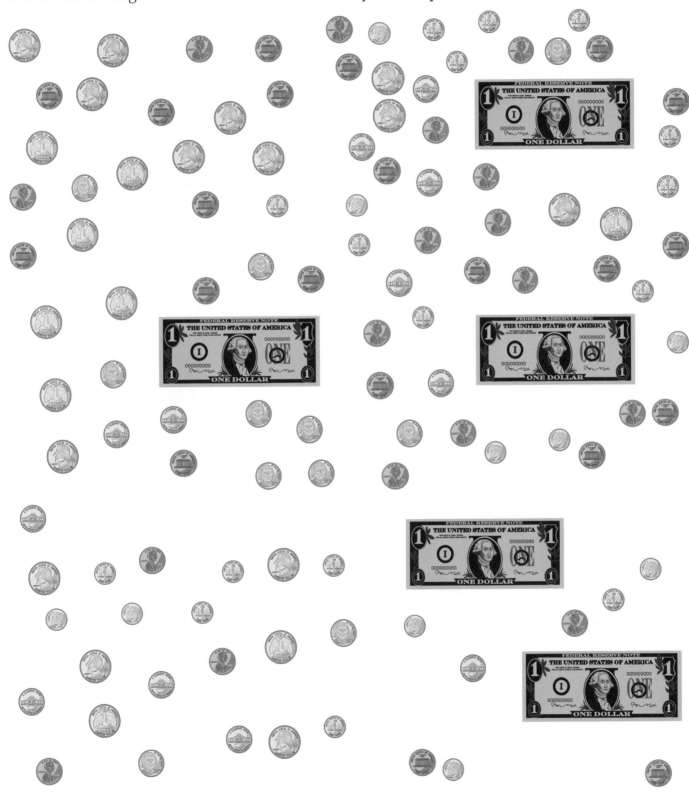

What's in My Hand?

READ the clues, and WRITE how many of each coin and bill are hidden in the hand.

I'm holding six paper bills and nine coins.

The money in my hand totals $48.89.

My coins total less than one dollar.

I don't have any 10-dollar bills.

What's in my hand?

1. _____ 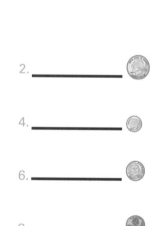   2. _____

3. _____   4. _____

5. _____   6. _____

7. _____   8. _____

Stamp Collector

DRAW lines to mark where you would tear the sheet of stamps to create three sheets of stamps of equal value.

HINT: The three sets do not need to contain the same number of stamps.

Big Spender

Rachel and Gabby went to a Sara Starlight concert together, and Rachel spent twice as much as Gabby. DRAW a circle around the things that Rachel bought and a square around the things that Gabby bought.

$25.00

$25.00

$35.00

$19.00

SODA

$2.75

$6.50

Fraction and Decimal Cards

CUT OUT the 24 cards.

These cards are for use with page 141. Use either the fraction side or the decimal side. (The two sides are not equivalent.)

✂

$\frac{1}{2}$	$\frac{1}{3}$	$\frac{2}{3}$	$\frac{1}{4}$
$\frac{3}{4}$	$\frac{1}{5}$	$\frac{2}{5}$	$\frac{3}{5}$
$\frac{4}{5}$	$\frac{1}{6}$	$\frac{5}{6}$	$\frac{1}{7}$
$\frac{2}{7}$	$\frac{3}{7}$	$\frac{4}{7}$	$\frac{5}{7}$
$\frac{6}{7}$	$\frac{1}{8}$	$\frac{3}{8}$	$\frac{5}{8}$
$\frac{7}{8}$	$\frac{1}{9}$	$\frac{4}{9}$	$\frac{8}{9}$

0.1	0.2	0.3	0.4
0.5	0.6	0.7	0.8
0.9	0.16	0.23	0.25
0.33	0.38	0.42	0.48
0.55	0.61	0.67	0.73
0.74	0.87	0.91	0.99

Pentominoes

CUT OUT the 13 pentomino pieces. (Cut along the black lines only.)

These pentomino pieces are for use with pages 155 and 157.

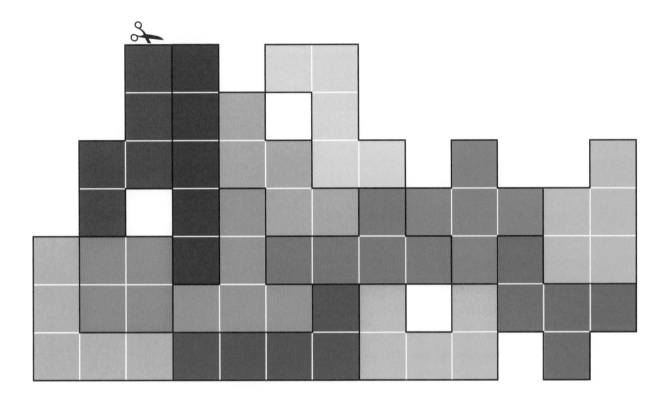

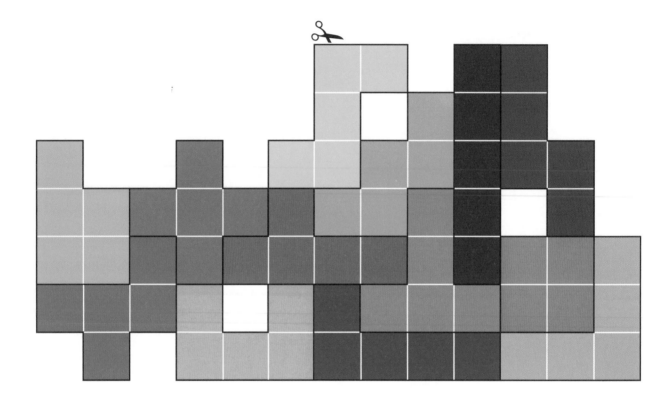

Tangrams

CUT OUT the seven tangram pieces.

These tangram pieces are for use with pages 175 and 176.

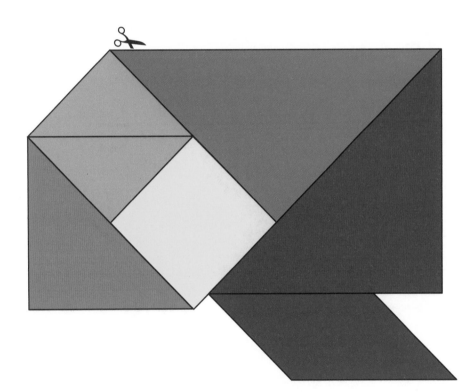

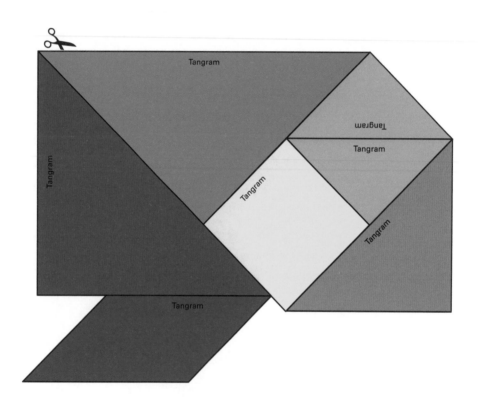

Pattern Blocks

CUT OUT the 31 pattern block pieces.

These pattern block pieces are for use with page 178.

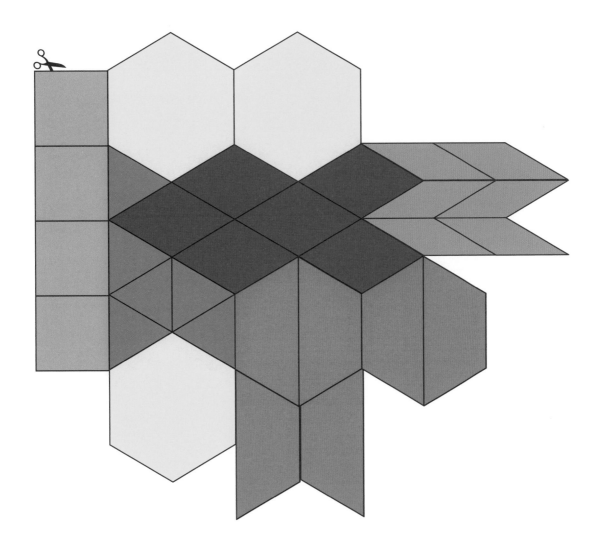

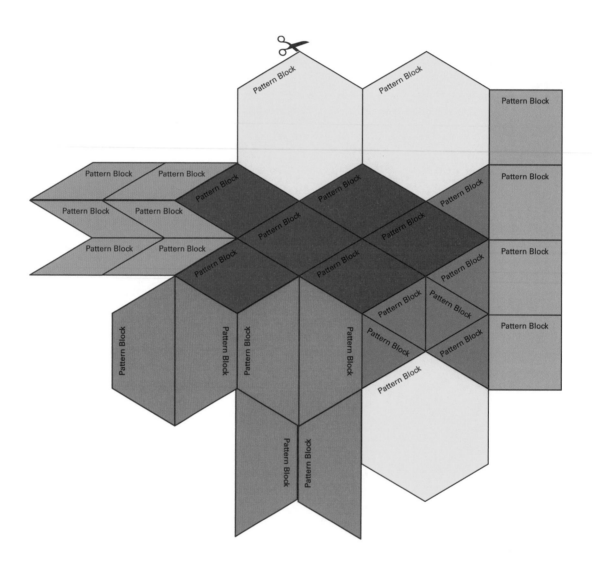

Page 105
1. 84,165
2. 4,672,244
3. 961,723
4. 29,811
5. 115,736
6. 2,082,641
7. 505,692
8. 3,937,260

2	9	8	1	1	0	0	2
9	5	0	5	6	9	2	0
8	1	8	2	4	6	7	8
2	4	4	9	9	1	3	2
0	5	1	1	5	7	3	6
3	4	6	7	2	2	4	4
6	0	5	3	7	3	4	1
3	9	3	7	2	6	0	8

Pages 106–107

2	5	9	1	3	2	4	

Page 108

7,138,605

Page 109

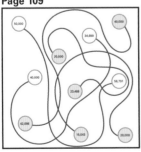

Page 110
1. 228,864
2. 341,156
3. 275,319
4. 384,620
5. 382,495
6. 392,382
7. 232,981
8. 337,236
9. 246,518

Page 111

Page 112
1. 5,237,564
2. 5,418,163
3. 5,908,752
4. 6,692,556
5. 6,694,204
6. 6,563,827
7. 5,879,215
8. 5,418,921
9. 5,826,138

Page 113
1. 27, 49, 80, 115
2. 0, 35, 66, 112
3. 106, 165, 240, 294

Page 114

1,839,617

Page 115
1. 21, 33, 45, 63
2. 2, 3, 6, 9
3. 4, 8, 14, 18

Page 116
6,818,567

Page 117

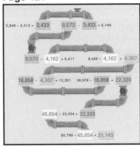

Pages 118–119

Page 120
1. 76,977
2. 85,543
3. 51,349
4. 59,868
5. 99,758
6. 62,372
7. 40,703
8. 71,230

4	0	7	0	3	6	5	7
1	3	9	8	5	2	2	6
0	9	9	5	1	3	4	9
8	6	7	0	4	7	9	7
5	4	4	7	9	2	0	7
5	9	8	6	8	3	1	5
4	9	2	7	1	2	3	0
3	1	1	4	0	8	7	4

Page 121

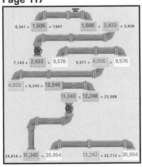

Pages 122–123

Page 124
1. 22,311
2. 76,213
3. 55,224
4. 71,018
5. 49,876
6. 18,236
7. 61,086
8. 34,972

1	8	2	3	6	9	6	1
7	6	2	4	6	0	1	7
1	1	0	2	3	5	0	1
3	5	5	2	2	4	8	0
4	2	2	3	5	9	6	1
9	0	4	1	6	8	1	8
7	6	2	1	3	7	6	2
2	9	8	3	3	6	7	2

Page 125

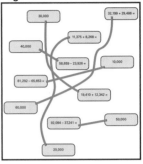

Page 126

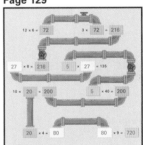

Page 127
1. 30
2. 16
3. 36
4. 25
5. 24
6. 60
7. 7
8. 72
9. 48
10. 18
11. 45
12. 40

WHEREVER YOU PUT HIM.

Page 128

	4	7
1	4	7
2	8	14

	5	6
1	5	6
3	15	18

	2	7
9	18	63
10	20	70

	5	8
2	10	16
6	30	48

	3	8
7	21	56
9	27	72

	5	6
7	35	42
9	45	54

Page 129

Pages 130–131

Answers

Page 132

13	×	11	=	143
×		×		×
6	×	14	=	84
=		=		=
78	×	154	=	12,012

Page 133
1. 7   2. 8   3. 10
4. 1   5. 4   6. 2
7. 5   8. 11   9. 3
10. 12   11. 6   12. 9
HE CAUGHT A LOT OF FLIES.

Page 134
1. 9, 2, 6, 8
2. 8, 3, 1, 7
3. 16, 4, 8, 10

Page 135
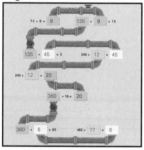

Pages 136–137

1	3	2		4	1	8
3	4	1		1	0	5
		0		9		
2	1				1	2
2	5	3		4	6	0
3	0				2	9
		3		5		
2	9	1		3	8	5
1	2	0		2	4	3

Page 138

972	÷	36	=	27
÷		÷		÷
54	÷	6	=	9
=		=		=
18	÷	6	=	3

Page 139
1. SU   2. M   3. ME
4. R   5. VAC   6. A
7. TI   8. ON
SUMMER VACATION

Page 140
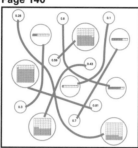

Page 141
Have someone check
your answers.

Page 142
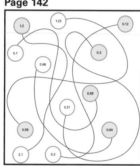

Page 143
1. $\frac{3}{4}$ 2. $\frac{5}{6}$ 3. $\frac{3}{3}$

4. $\frac{5}{9}$ 5. $\frac{7}{8}$ 6. $\frac{2}{5}$

7. $\frac{2}{3}$ 8. $\frac{5}{7}$ 9. $\frac{5}{8}$
THE LIBRARY.

Page 144
1. $\frac{2}{7}, \frac{4}{7}, \frac{6}{7}, \frac{7}{7}$

2. $\frac{3}{9}, \frac{5}{9}, \frac{6}{9}, \frac{8}{9}$

3. $\frac{7}{10}, \frac{8}{10}, \frac{10}{10}, \frac{12}{10}$

Page 145
1. $\frac{2}{5}$ 2. $\frac{7}{12}$ 3. $\frac{3}{8}$

4. $\frac{1}{3}$ 5. $\frac{3}{6}$ 6. $\frac{1}{7}$

7. $\frac{1}{4}$ 8. $\frac{3}{5}$ 9. $\frac{2}{9}$

10. $\frac{2}{11}$ 11. $\frac{5}{6}$ 12. $\frac{3}{10}$

THEY USE THEIR SHELL
PHONES.

Page 146
1. $\frac{1}{6}, \frac{2}{6}, \frac{3}{6}, \frac{4}{6}$

2. $\frac{1}{8}, \frac{3}{8}, \frac{5}{8}, \frac{6}{8}$

3. $\frac{1}{12}, \frac{4}{12}, \frac{6}{12}, \frac{8}{12}$

Page 147
1. 9.7   2. 3.5
3. 3.81   4. 8.47
5. 8.02   6. 10.19
7. 6.1   8. 5.6
9. 4.43   10. 1.84
11. 2.93
TIME TO GET A NEW TABLE.

Page 148
1. 2.1, 2.5, 3.4, 4.3
2. 5.69, 6.2, 9.75, 12.18
3. 8.71, 12.59, 16.91, 26.47

Page 149
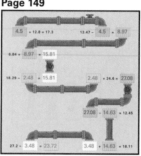

Page 150
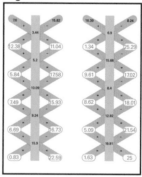

Page 151
A FENCE.

Page 152
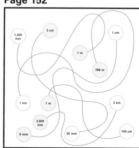

Page 153
A JUNKYARD.

Page 154
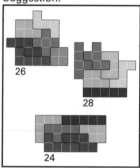

Page 155
Suggestion:
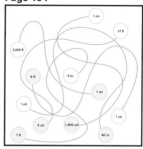

26

28

24

Page 156
Have someone check your
answers.

Page 157
Suggestion:
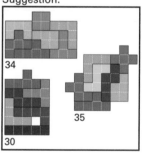

34

35

30

Page 158
Have someone check
your answers.

Page 159
1. 5,000   2. 2.3   3. 6,000
4. 0.6   5. 3   6. 6,500
7. 1,500   8. 10.4   9. 200
10. 1
YOU CAN ADD A HOLE.

Page 160
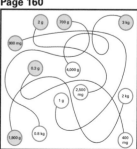

Page 161

1. 2
2. $1\frac{1}{2}$
3. 32
4. 500
5. 6,000
6. $2\frac{1}{2}$
7. 1
8. 12
9. 8
10. 5,500

THEY BOTH WEIGH ONE TON.

Page 162

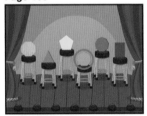

Page 163

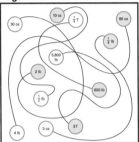

Pages 164–165

Pages 166–168
Have someone check your answers.

Page 169

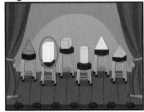

Page 170

Page 171
Have someone check your answers.

Page 172

1. cube
2. square pyramid
3. square pyramid
4. 6
5. 5

Page 175
Suggestion:

Page 176
Suggestion:

Page 177

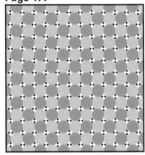

Page 178

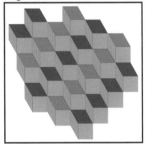

Page 179
144

Page 180
81

Page 181

Page 182

Page 183

Pages 184–185

1. IRELAND
2. SPAIN
3. ITALY
4. NORWAY
5. BELARUS
6. FRANCE
7. GERMANY
FINLAND

Page 186

Page 187

1. unlikely
2. impossible
3. certain

Page 188

1. $\frac{1}{8}$
2. $\frac{1}{2}$
3. impossible
4. unlikely
5. certain

Page 191
12 (1:11, 2:22, 3:33, 4:44, 5:55, 11:11, both a.m. and p.m.)

Pages 192–193

1. 41
2. 68
3. 75
4. 19

Page 194
22 (Clock hands pass each other around the times 1:06, 2:11, 3:17, 4:22, 5:27, 6:33, 7:38, 8:43, 9:49, 10:55, and 12:00 twice per day.)

Page 195

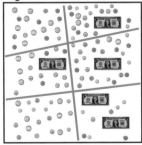

Answers

Page 196

1. 2 2. 3
3. 0 4. 0
5. 1 6. 2
7. 3 8. 4

Page 197

Page 198

4th Grade
Math in Action

Building the Band

WRITE the number for each number word used in the paragraph.

David, Hina, Sara, and Maxwell are in a band called Space Portal. Space Portal has played a lot of local shows, but the largest audience they've ever had has been four thousand, nine hundred sixty-five people. Maxwell decided to make flyers to promote the band. He and the band put ten thousand, five hundred fifteen flyers up around all the nearby towns. After that, they had as many as nine thousand, one hundred seventy-three people at their shows. They wanted to think bigger. Hina made a Space Portal Web site and sent the link to twenty-one thousand, three hundred forty other music sites. Before long, one hundred twenty-four thousand, six hundred three people had visited the Web site. Now Space Portal is at the top of the charts, and they play sold-out shows for as many as seventy-six thousand, nine-hundred forty-two people. Each month, the Space Portal Web site has an average of one million, eight hundred two thousand, one hundred ninety-nine visitors.

1. 4,965 _____

2. _____

3. _____

4. _____

5. _____

6. _____

7. _____

Place Value

Check This Out

To write a check, the amount of the check must be written as both a number and number words. WRITE the number words missing from each check.

1.

Ruby Moneypenny   545

Date February 1, 2010

Pay to the Order of Audrey's Jewelry Store $ 3,297

_____ Dollars

Memo _____

A560000056A10209443322O5C 545

2.

Tami Hagar   322

Date April 20, 2010

Pay to the Order of Crazy Carl's Cars $ 48,158

_____ Dollars

Memo _____

A320000032A10305646745C 322

3.

Summer Brown   1062

Date August 15, 2010

Pay to the Order of Collegiate College $ 105,366

_____ Dollars

Memo _____

A650000065A20205436185C 1062

4.

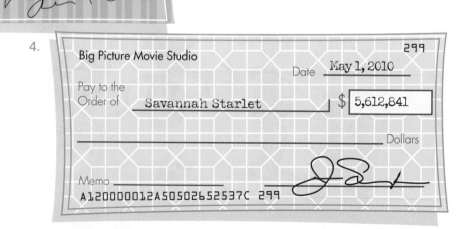

Big Picture Movie Studio   299

Date May 1, 2010

Pay to the Order of Savannah Starlet $ 5,612,841

_____ Dollars

Memo _____

A120000012A50502652537C 299

Piggy Bank

Each row shows money in and out of the piggy bank. CIRCLE the larger amount.

$4,008

$6,046

$8,154

$4,781

$9,490

Big Lakes

The approximate area of each lake is shown in square kilometers. WRITE the numbers 1 through 10 so that 1 is the largest lake and 10 is the smallest lake.

1. Lake Michigan, North America   57,800 sq km   _____

2. Great Bear Lake, North America   31,300 sq km   _____

3. Lake Tanganyika, Africa   32,600 sq km   _____

4. Lake Superior, North America   82,100 sq km   _____

5. Lake Ladoga, Europe   17,700 sq km   _____

6. Lake Huron, North America   59,600 sq km   _____

7. Lake Malawi, Africa   28,900 sq km   _____

8. Lake Victoria, Africa   69,500 sq km   _____

9. Lake Baikal, Asia   31,500 sq km   _____

10. Lake Erie, North America   25,700 sq km   _____

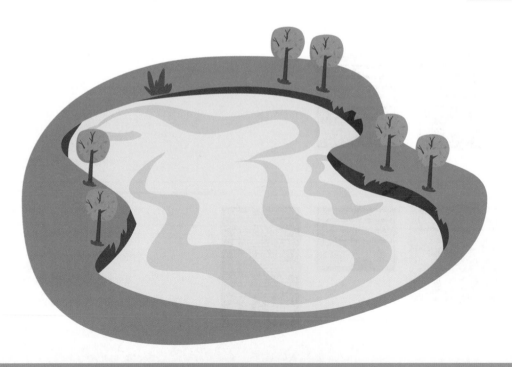

2

City Stats

The **population** of a place is the number of people living there. CIRCLE the name of the city in each row with the largest population.

1. New Orleans
    United States
    476,600

    Benxi
    China
    937,800

    Athens
    Greece
    772,100

2. Lyon
    France
    415,000

    Dublin
    Ireland
    481,900

    Denver
    United States
    497,800

3. Lisbon
    Portugal
    663,400

    Seville
    Spain
    697,500

    Nasik
    India
    656,900

4. Kuala Lumpur
    Malaysia
    1,145,100

    Sofia
    Bulgaria
    1,116,800

    Daqing
    China
    1,177,000

5. Minsk
    Belarus
    1,671,600

    Cali
    Columbia
    1,666,500

    Warsaw
    Poland
    1,632,500

6. Lima
    Peru
    5,681,900

    New York
    United States
    7,380,900

    Cairo
    Egypt
    6,800,000

Tourist Traps

LOOK at the average number of visitors per year to each attraction. WRITE the numbers 1 through 10 so that 1 is the most visited attraction and 10 is the least visited attraction.

1. Grand Canyon   4,400,000 average yearly visitors _____

2. Navy Pier, Chicago   8,600,000 average yearly visitors _____

3. Delaware Water Gap   4,800,000 average yearly visitors _____

4. Universal Studios, Orlando   6,200,000 average yearly visitors _____

5. Hawaii Volcanoes National Park   1,200,000 average yearly visitors _____

6. Great Smoky Mountains National Park   9,400,000 average yearly visitors _____

7. Metropolitan Museum, New York   4,500,000 average yearly visitors _____

8. San Antonio River Walk   5,100,000 average yearly visitors _____

9. Sea World, San Diego   4,300,000 average yearly visitors _____

10. Yosemite National Park   3,300,000 average yearly visitors _____

Toy Builders

Four artists have each made a sculpture using only plastic toy bricks. ROUND the number of toy bricks each artist has used to the nearest ten thousand.

HINT: Numbers that end in 1 through 4,999 get rounded down to the nearest ten thousand, and numbers that end in 5,000 through 9,999 get rounded up to the nearest ten thousand.

1.

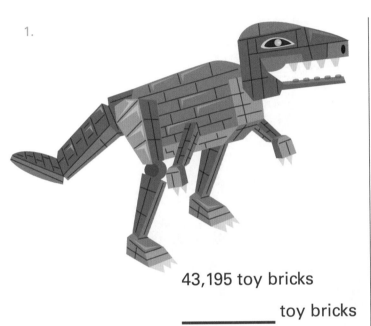

43,195 toy bricks

_____ toy bricks

2.

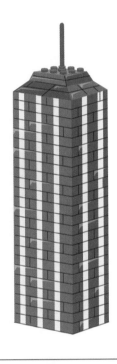

28,561 toy bricks

_____ toy bricks

3.

64,459 toy bricks

_____ toy bricks

4.

45,882 toy bricks

_____ toy bricks

Air Traffic Control

Air traffic controllers are looking at the number of flights that took off and landed at several airports last year to make a plan for the coming year. ROUND the number of flights at each airport to the nearest hundred thousand.

HINT: Numbers that end in 1 through 49,999 get rounded down to the nearest hundred thousand, and numbers that end in 50,000 through 99,999 get rounded up to the nearest hundred thousand.

1. Popperville Airport   324,736 flights   _____ flights

2. Indira International Airport   875,109 flights   _____ flights

3. Lambertville Airport   96,288 flights   _____ flights

4. Springfield International Airport   772,012 flights   _____ flights

5. Taft National Airport   538,524 flights   _____ flights

6. Smith Eastern Airport   662,003 flights   _____ flights

7. New City Airport   957,337 flights   _____ flights

8. Washington Airport   846,943 flights   _____ flights

Best Estimates

CIRCLE the best estimate.

1. About how many students can fit on a school bus?

   48   480   4,800

2. About how many apples can grow on one apple tree in a year?

   70   700   7,000

3. About how many seats are in a major-league baseball stadium?

   500   5,000   50,000

4. About how many minutes are in one day?

   140   1,400   14,000

5. About how many countries are there in the world?

   19   190   1,900

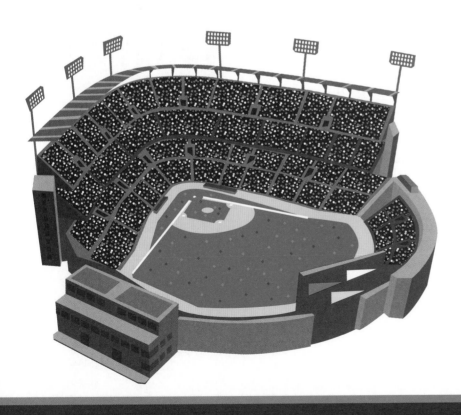

Empire State Building

The Empire State Building is a landmark building easily spotted in New York City's skyline. The building was completed in 1931, then the tallest building in the world at 102 stories tall. WRITE an estimate for each fact about the Empire State Building. CHECK page 305 to see how close your estimates were.

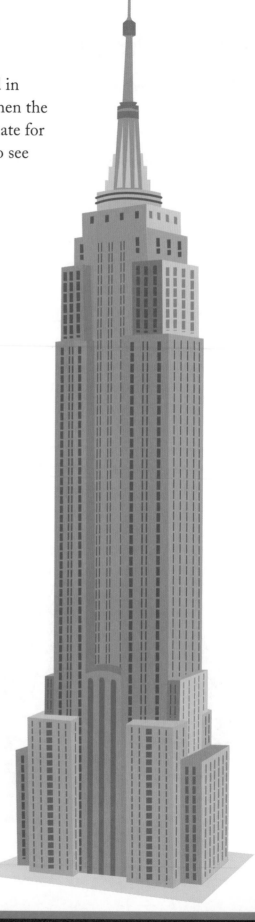

1. Number of elevators:

   Estimate: _____ Check: _____

2. Number of steps to the top floor:

   Estimate: _____ Check: _____

3. Number of windows:

   Estimate: _____ Check: _____

4. Number of bricks:

   Estimate: _____ Check: _____

5. Number of states you can see from the top of the building on a clear day (including New York):

   Estimate: _____ Check: _____

The Votes Are In

There are five candidates in a close race for mayor. The votes from the morning had already been counted, and now the afternoon votes have been counted as well. WRITE the total number of votes for each candidate, and circle the new mayor.

	Candidate 1	Candidate 2	Candidate 3	Candidate 4	Candidate 5
Morning votes	44,117	30,051	53,412	34,160	27,321
Afternoon votes	23,710	42,042	21,473	35,113	41,220
Total votes					

Plus Tax

The cost of expensive items gets even more expensive when you add sales tax. WRITE the total cost of each purchase.

1.

Price	$13,874
Tax	$ 1,109
Total	$

2.

Price	$39,895
Tax	$ 2,593
Total	$

3.

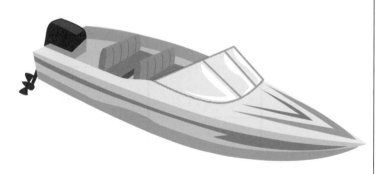

Price	$24,062
Tax	$ 1,684
Total	$

4.

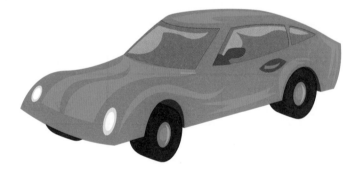

Price	$91,670
Tax	$ 5,959
Total	$

Larger Libraries

The state has provided money for each library to get a large number of new books. WRITE the number of books each library will have once the new books are purchased.

1. Howard Library

$$27,993 \text{ books}$$
$$+15,043 \text{ new books}$$

2. Park Hill Library

$$35,510 \text{ books}$$
$$+11,940 \text{ new books}$$

3. Crowell Library

$$23,438 \text{ books}$$
$$+19,779 \text{ new books}$$

4. Melrose Library

$$48,912 \text{ books}$$
$$+16,095 \text{ new books}$$

5. Gering Library

$$34,608 \text{ books}$$
$$+15,106 \text{ new books}$$

6. Wyndmere Library

$$49,532 \text{ books}$$
$$+18,841 \text{ new books}$$

That Does Not Compute!

The Great Roboto is on the fritz and is spitting out some math problems with wrong answers. CIRCLE the incorrect sums.

62,699
+12,218
(75,936)

35,480
+39,373
74,853

31,954
+18,337
50,291

42,382
+17,348
59,844

26,175
+12,083
40,258

70,718
+19,829
90,547

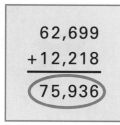

68,153
+28,188
96,341

57,964
+20,728
79,682

78,782
+13,535
85,517

45,286
+33,939
59,225

55,947
+25,493
81,440

81,097
+18,896
99,993

Best Price

Jada is shopping around for the best price on a used car. Each car dealer has a similar car for a different price, and each is offering cash back on the purchase. CIRCLE the car with the best price after the cash back is subtracted.

While Supplies Last

Radio station WTJT is having a giveaway every day during the morning radio show. They'll give away prizes to the first callers until they're gone. WRITE the number of callers for each giveaway that will not get a prize.

1. On Monday, 29,571 people called in to get one of WTJT's 16,520 station T-shirts. How many callers did not get a T-shirt? _____

2. On Tuesday, WTJT had 23,925 concert tickets to give away, and 32,428 people called in.
How many callers did not get a concert ticket? _____

3. On Wednesday, WTJT was giving away 28,355 CDs, and 40,010 people called in to get one.
How many callers did not get a CD? _____

4. On Thursday, 27,038 people called in to get one of the 22,512 restaurant gift certificates WTJT was giving away.
How many callers did not get a gift certificate? _____

5. Friday was the big giveaway. WTJT had 35,928 of the latest MP3 players, and 56,247 people called in to get one.
How many callers did not get an MP3 player? _____

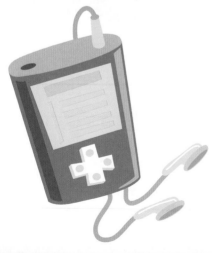

Wide Worlds

The chart shows the width of each planet at its widest point.
LOOK at the chart, and ANSWER the questions.

Planet	Width at Widest Point
Mercury	3,032 miles
Venus	7,521 miles
Earth	7,926 miles
Mars	4,222 miles
Jupiter	88,846 miles
Saturn	74,898 miles
Uranus	31,763 miles
Neptune	30,775 miles

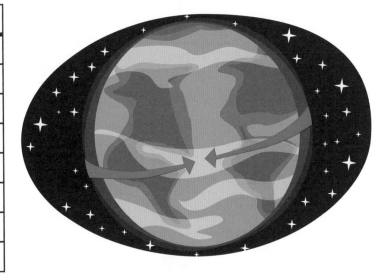

1. How much wider is Earth than Mercury? _____ miles

2. How much wider is Neptune than Mars? _____ miles

3. How much wider is Jupiter than Saturn? _____ miles

4. How much wider is Uranus than Venus? _____ miles

5. How much wider is Earth than Venus? _____ miles

6. How much wider is Saturn than Neptune? _____ miles

7. How much wider is Mars than Mercury? _____ miles

8. How much wider is Jupiter than Uranus? _____ miles

That Does Not Compute!

The Great Roboto is on the fritz and is spitting out some math problems with wrong answers. CIRCLE the incorrect differences.

$$23,350 - 12,907 = 11,453$$

$$39,166 - 23,735 = 15,431$$

$$83,798 - 79,676 = 14,122$$

$$54,438 - 13,997 = 40,441$$

$$50,038 - 21,611 = 38,627$$

$$91,711 - 44,180 = 47,531$$

$$87,273 - 27,318 = 69,955$$

$$48,367 - 45,712 = 2,655$$

$$91,081 - 24,007 = 67,086$$

$$47,540 - 15,917 = 31,623$$

$$73,391 - 46,384 = 27,007$$

$$53,138 - 35,494 = 22,644$$

Candy Factory

ESTIMATE each sum or difference by rounding to the nearest ten thousand.

1. The candy factory made 42,820 Chocolate Crunch Clusters one week and 51,790 Chocolate Crunch Clusters the next week. About how many Chocolate Crunch Clusters were made? _____

2. The candy factory made 67,208 Gum Chewies and packaged and shipped 32,986. About how many Gum Chewies remain at the factory? _____

3. The candy factory made 24,641 Coconutties and 35,187 Coconut Twists. About how many coconut-flavored candies were made altogether? _____

4. The candy factory made 68,125 Cherry Juicies. Because of an equipment problem, 16,921 were not injected with cherry juice and had to be thrown away. About how many Cherry Juicies are left? _____

5. The candy factory made 14,018 Peanut Buddies, 47,259 Peanutties, and 23,432 Peanut Butter Beans. About how many peanut-flavored candies were made altogether? _____

6. The candy factory made 92,450 Lemon Lickers and gave 48,376 of them to nearby hospitals. About how many Lemon Lickers did the factory have left? _____

Calculator Catch

Calculators can be a great help in solving problems if you push the right buttons. ESTIMATE each sum or difference by rounding to the nearest ten thousand. COMPARE the estimates with the number on the calculator, and CIRCLE the calculators showing the wrong answers.

61,265
+10,942

60,000
+10,000

70,000

64,427
−33,158

−

26,723
+24,304

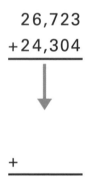

+

88,595
−16,913

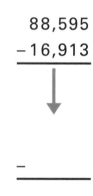

−

48,126
+39,591

+

72,088
−63,213

−

High Score

These four kids are all trying to get the high score in a video game where they earn points by collecting gems. MULTIPLY the gems by the correct number of points. Then ADD the scores, and CIRCLE the person with the highest score.

= 6 points   = 7 points   = 8 points   = 9 points   = 10 points

Player 1	
4 ×	
5 ×	
9 ×	
0 ×	
2 ×	
Total Score	

Player 2	
10 ×	
2 ×	
3 ×	
7 ×	
4 ×	
Total Score	

Player 3	
5 ×	
9 ×	
8 ×	
8 ×	
0 ×	
Total Score	

Player 4	
3 ×	
10 ×	
1 ×	
2 ×	
3 ×	
Total Score	

Excellent Exercise

WRITE the number of times each person did each exercise.

Rita did nine sets of 5 jumping jacks, six sets of 8 sit-ups, five sets of 5 push-ups, and two sets of 10 pull-ups. How many times did Rita do each exercise?

George did four sets of 8 jumping jacks, three sets of 10 sit-ups, six sets of 6 push-ups, and four sets of 7 pull-ups. How many times did George do each exercise?

_____ jumping jacks   _____ sit-ups
1   2

_____ push-ups   _____ pull-ups
3   4

_____ jumping jacks   _____ sit-ups
5   6

_____ push-ups   _____ pull-ups
7   8

Amy did seven sets of 5 jumping jacks, eight sets of 9 sit-ups, two sets of 10 push-ups, and two sets of 8 pull-ups. How many times did Amy do each exercise?

Marco did five sets of 10 jumping jacks, four sets of 6 sit-ups, nine sets of 5 push-ups, and three sets of 8 pull-ups. How many times did Marco do each exercise?

_____ jumping jacks   _____ sit-ups
9   10

_____ push-ups   _____ pull-ups
11   12

_____ jumping jacks   _____ sit-ups
13   14

_____ push-ups   _____ pull-ups
15   16

Walkathon

Charlie and Simone are participating in a walkathon to raise money for cancer research, and they are working together to collect donations. WRITE the amount of each type of donation they raised.

1. Seven people gave Charlie and Simone donations of $20. $ 140

2. Three people gave Charlie and Simone donations of $25. $

3. Six people gave Charlie and Simone donations of $30. $

4. Nine people gave Charlie and Simone donations of $35. $

5. Two people gave Charlie and Simone donations of $40. $

6. Eight people gave Charlie and Simone donations of $45. $

7. Four people gave Charlie and Simone donations of $50. $

8. Five people gave Charlie and Simone donations of $55. $

9. Six people gave Charlie and Simone donations of $60. $

10. Three people gave Charlie and Simone donations of $65. $

11. Seven people gave Charlie and Simone donations of $70. $

12. Nine people gave Charlie and Simone donations of $75. $

Air Traffic Control

Each airport handles a different number of flights per hour during the peak morning hours of 6 a.m. to 10 a.m. and the peak afternoon hours of 3 p.m. to 8 p.m. WRITE the total number of flights for each airport during the four-hour morning rush and the five-hour afternoon rush.

	Flights per Hour	Total Morning Flights	Total Afternoon Flights
1. Popperville Airport	90	_____	_____
2. Indira International Airport	75	_____	_____
3. Lambertville Airport	32	_____	_____
4. Springfield International Airport	88	_____	_____
5. Taft National Airport	64	_____	_____
6. Smith Eastern Airport	51	_____	_____
7. New City Airport	82	_____	_____
8. Washington Airport	77	_____	_____

Counting Calories

The nutrition information on a food package shows the number of calories per serving, but there is often more than one serving in a package. WRITE the total number of calories in each package.

1.

Nutrition Facts

Serving Size 4 cookies
Servings Per Container 9

Amount Per Serving
Calories 175

Total Calories _____

2.

Nutrition Facts

Serving Size $\frac{1}{2}$ cup
Servings Per Container 4

Amount Per Serving
Calories 270

Total Calories _____

3.

Nutrition Facts

Serving Size $\frac{1}{2}$ cup
Servings Per Container 8

Amount Per Serving
Calories 55

Total Calories _____

4.

Nutrition Facts

Serving Size 15 pieces
Servings Per Container 9

Amount Per Serving
Calories 140

Total Calories _____

5.

Nutrition Facts

Serving Size $\frac{1}{2}$ of package
Servings Per Container 2

Amount Per Serving
Calories 216

Total Calories _____

6.

Nutrition Facts

Serving Size 2 oz
Servings Per Container 8

Amount Per Serving
Calories 230

Total Calories _____

Food Factories

Each factory can make a large number of food products per hour. WRITE the number of food products that can be made in an eight-hour shift.

1. The peanut-butter factory can make 410 jars of peanut butter in one hour.

   In eight hours the factory can make _____ jars of peanut butter.

2. The bread factory can make 185 loaves of bread in one hour.

   In eight hours the factory can make _____ loaves of bread.

3. The marshmallow factory can make 122 bags of marshmallows in one hour.

   In eight hours the factory can make _____ bags of marshmallows.

4. The bubblegum factory can make 999 pieces of bubblegum in one hour.

   In eight hours the factory can make _____ pieces of bubblegum.

5. The applesauce factory can make 384 jars of applesauce in one hour.

   In eight hours the factory can make _____ jars of applesauce.

6. The potato chip factory can make 339 bags of potato chips in one hour.

   In eight hours the factory can make _____ bags of potato chips.

7. The yogurt factory can make 741 containers of yogurt in one hour.

   In eight hours the factory can make _____ containers of yogurt.

8. The ice cream factory can make 245 pints of ice cream in one hour.

   In eight hours the factory can make _____ pints of ice cream.

High Score

WRITE the number of gems each player collected based on the final scores.

🔹 = 6 points 🔸 = 7 points 🔹 = 8 points 🔹 = 9 points 🔹 = 10 points

Player 1		
	× 🔹	36
	× 🔹	35
	× 🔹	16
	× 🔹	90
	× 🔹	10
Total Score		187

Player 2		
	× 🔹	54
	× 🔹	21
	× 🔹	56
	× 🔹	18
	× 🔹	100
Total Score		249

Player 3		
	× 🔹	42
	× 🔹	28
	× 🔹	48
	× 🔹	27
	× 🔹	20
Total Score		165

Player 4		
	× 🔹	24
	× 🔹	63
	× 🔹	64
	× 🔹	9
	× 🔹	50
Total Score		210

Best Price

For each set of books, WRITE the cost of one book. Then CIRCLE the set of books that has the lowest cost per book.

6 books for $54

$_____ per book

1

7 books for $49

$_____ per book

2

8 books for $40

$_____ per book

3

3 books for $24

$_____ per book

4

4 books for $24

$_____ per book

5

7 books for $63

$_____ per book

6

5 books for $25

$_____ per book

7

2 books for $14

$_____ per book

8

10 books for $40

$_____ per book

9

Save the Day

The Masked Maven has been rounding up villains all over Urbanopolis and filling all of the city jails. WRITE the number of villains that will be in each crowded jail cell.

1. The Masked Maven brought 45 villains to City Penitentiary, which has three available jail cells.

   There will be _____ villains in each jail cell.

2. The Masked Maven dropped off 84 villains at Urbanopolis Jail, which has seven available jail cells.

   There will be _____ villains in each jail cell.

3. The Masked Maven unloaded 95 villains at Urbanopolis North Prison, which has five available jail cells.

   There will be _____ villains in each jail cell.

4. There will be 56 villains crowded into the two available cells at the Downtown Correctional Facility, thanks to the Masked Maven.

   There will be _____ villains in each jail cell.

5. The Masked Maven brought 88 villains to City Lockup, which has four available jail cells.

   There will be _____ villains in each jail cell.

6. The South Slammer has 96 villains for its six available jail cells, courtesy of the Masked Maven.

   There will be _____ villains in each jail cell.

Gassing Up

A car is more fuel-efficient than another car when it can drive more miles on a gallon of gas. WRITE the miles per gallon (mpg) for each car. Then CIRCLE the most fuel-efficient car.

HINT: Divide the miles driven by the gallons of gas used, and the quotient will be the miles per gallon.

1. This car drove 144 miles on six gallons of gas. _____ mpg

2. This car drove 153 miles on nine gallons of gas. _____ mpg

3. This car drove 248 miles on eight gallons of gas. _____ mpg

4. This car drove 110 miles on five gallons of gas. _____ mpg

5. This car drove 128 miles on four gallons of gas. _____ mpg

6. This car drove 175 miles on seven gallons of gas. _____ mpg

Pay the Check

Four people are chipping in to pay each restaurant check. WRITE the amount each person will pay if they split the cost equally.

1.

GUEST CHECK		
Date	Table	Guests	Server	**00845**
Orzo with shrimp		$ 35
Pork medallions		$ 32
Hanger steak		$ 43
Roasted lemon chicken		$ 30
	Total	$140

$_____ per person

2.

GUEST CHECK		
Date	Table	Guests	Server	**00846**
Cheese enchiladas		$13
Chicken quesadilla		$14
Fajita fiesta		$20
Beef chimichanga		$17
	Total	$64

$_____ per person

3.

GUEST CHECK		
Date	Table	Guests	Server	**00847**
Ricotta gnocchi		$ 32
Spaghetti alla carbonara		$ 25
Clam linguine		$ 29
Lamb short ribs		$ 38
	Total	$124

$_____ per person

Bus Trip

Several schools are planning to send students to the state science fair. If each bus can hold 48 students, WRITE the number of buses each school will need to get its students to the science fair.

1. Edison Elementary School is sending 288 students to the science fair. _____ buses

2. Curie Elementary School is sending 192 students to the science fair. _____ buses

3. Darwin Elementary School is sending 624 students to the science fair. _____ buses

4. Tesla Elementary School is sending 432 students to the science fair. _____ buses

5. Newton Elementary School is sending 576 students to the science fair. _____ buses

6. Galilei Elementary School is sending 480 students to the science fair. _____ buses

7. Albert Elementary School is sending 384 students to the science fair. _____ buses

8. Locke Elementary School is sending 720 students to the science fair. _____ buses

Leftover Pizza

WRITE the fraction of each pizza that hasn't been eaten.

1. This pizza was cut into 8 slices, and 5 slices were eaten.

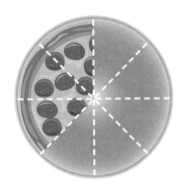

___

2. This pizza was cut into 6 slices, and 1 slice was eaten.

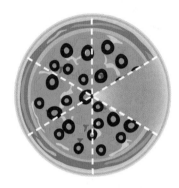

___

3. This pizza was cut into 7 slices, and 6 slices were eaten.

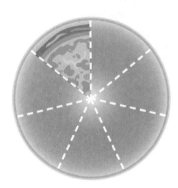

___

4. This pizza was cut into 9 slices, and 7 slices were eaten.

___

5. This pizza was cut into 4 slices, and 1 slice was eaten.

___

6. This pizza was cut into 12 slices, and 7 slices were eaten.

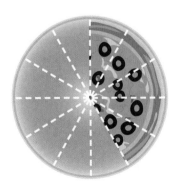

___

Skateboard Sort

WRITE each fraction.

1. Fraction of striped skateboards   —

2. Fraction of skateboards with animals   —

3. Fraction of skateboards with blue wheels   —

4. Fraction of skateboards with flames   —

5. Fraction of skateboards with green wheels   —

6. Fraction of black skateboards   —

More Chocolate for Me

CIRCLE the largest fraction of the chocolate bar in each row.

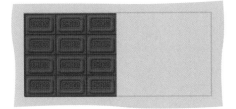

$$\frac{1}{2}$$

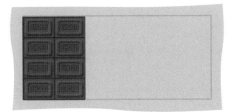

$$\frac{1}{3}$$

$$\frac{1}{4}$$

$$\frac{3}{4}$$

$$\frac{5}{6}$$

$$\frac{2}{3}$$

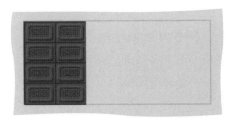

$$\frac{2}{6}$$

$$\frac{1}{4}$$

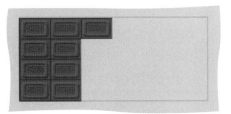

$$\frac{3}{8}$$

$$\frac{5}{12}$$

$$\frac{5}{8}$$

$$\frac{3}{6}$$

Kate's Kitchen

Today in Kate's Kitchen, Kate is making similar recipes for apple muffins. COMPARE the three recipes. For each ingredient, CIRCLE the largest fraction among the three recipes.

Kate's Apple Muffins

$\frac{3}{4}$ cup flour

$\frac{1}{4}$ cup sugar

$\frac{1}{2}$ cup brown sugar

$\frac{1}{2}$ teaspoon cinnamon

$\frac{1}{3}$ cup butter

$\frac{3}{4}$ cup chopped apples

1 egg

Yummy Apple Muffins

$\frac{5}{6}$ cup flour

$\frac{1}{8}$ cup sugar

$\frac{1}{3}$ cup brown sugar

$\frac{1}{3}$ teaspoon cinnamon

$\frac{3}{4}$ cup butter

$\frac{1}{2}$ cup chopped apples

2 eggs

Mom's Apple Muffins

$\frac{1}{2}$ cup flour

$\frac{1}{3}$ cup sugar

$\frac{2}{5}$ cup brown sugar

$\frac{1}{4}$ teaspoon cinnamon

$\frac{2}{3}$ cup butter

$\frac{7}{8}$ cup chopped apples

1 egg

Leftover Pizza

WRITE the fraction of pizza that can be made if two people combine their leftover pizza.

1.
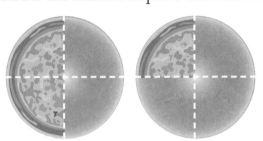

$$\frac{2}{4} \quad + \quad \frac{1}{4} \quad = \quad \underline{\quad}$$

2.
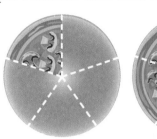

$$\frac{1}{5} \quad + \quad \frac{3}{5} \quad = \quad \underline{\quad}$$

3.
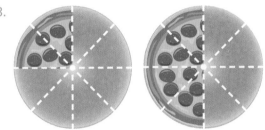

$$\frac{2}{8} \quad + \quad \frac{4}{8} \quad = \quad \underline{\quad}$$

4.
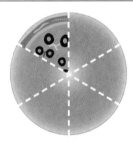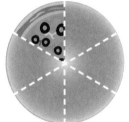

$$\frac{1}{6} \quad + \quad \frac{1}{6} \quad = \quad \underline{\quad}$$

5.
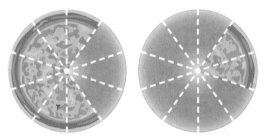

$$\frac{7}{10} \quad + \quad \frac{2}{10} \quad = \quad \underline{\quad}$$

6.

$$\frac{2}{7} \quad + \quad \frac{2}{7} \quad = \quad \underline{\quad}$$

7.
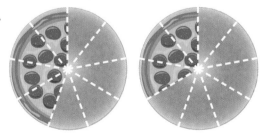

$$\frac{4}{9} \quad + \quad \frac{3}{9} \quad = \quad$$

8.
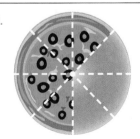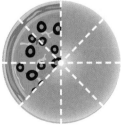

$$\frac{5}{8} \quad + \quad \frac{3}{8} \quad = \quad \underline{\quad}$$

Kate's Kitchen

Today in Kate's Kitchen, Kate is showing how to double a recipe. WRITE the new amount of each ingredient in the doubled recipe.

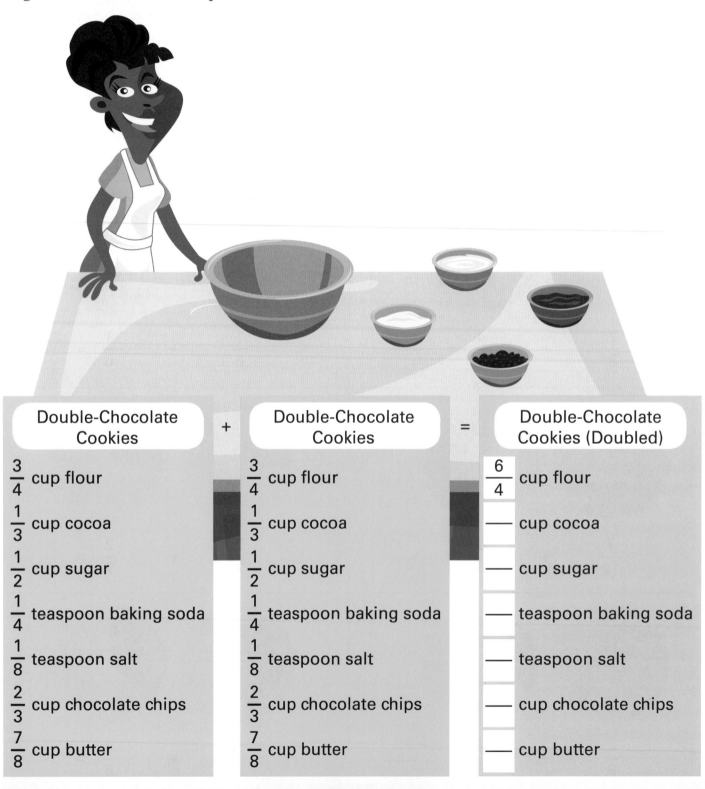

Double-Chocolate Cookies	+	Double-Chocolate Cookies	=	Double-Chocolate Cookies (Doubled)
$\frac{3}{4}$ cup flour		$\frac{3}{4}$ cup flour		$\frac{6}{4}$ cup flour
$\frac{1}{3}$ cup cocoa		$\frac{1}{3}$ cup cocoa		— cup cocoa
$\frac{1}{2}$ cup sugar		$\frac{1}{2}$ cup sugar		— cup sugar
$\frac{1}{4}$ teaspoon baking soda		$\frac{1}{4}$ teaspoon baking soda		— teaspoon baking soda
$\frac{1}{8}$ teaspoon salt		$\frac{1}{8}$ teaspoon salt		— teaspoon salt
$\frac{2}{3}$ cup chocolate chips		$\frac{2}{3}$ cup chocolate chips		— cup chocolate chips
$\frac{7}{8}$ cup butter		$\frac{7}{8}$ cup butter		— cup butter

Louisa's Lasagna

WRITE the fraction of lasagna that's left after some has been eaten.

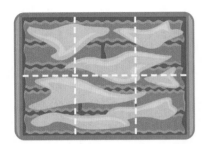

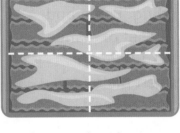

1. Louisa cut her lasagna into 6 pieces, and 4 pieces were eaten.

$$\frac{6}{6} - \frac{4}{6} = \underline{\quad}$$

2. Louisa cut her lasagna into 4 pieces, and 1 piece was eaten.

$$\frac{4}{4} - \frac{1}{4} = \underline{\quad}$$

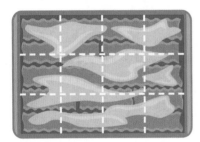

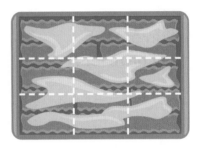

3. Louisa cut her lasagna into 12 pieces, and 7 pieces were eaten.

$$\frac{12}{12} - \frac{7}{12} = \underline{\quad}$$

4. Louisa cut her lasagna into 9 pieces, and 5 pieces were eaten.

$$\frac{9}{9} - \frac{5}{9} = \underline{\quad}$$

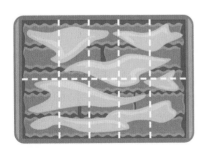

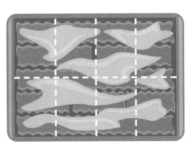

5. Louisa cut her lasagna into 10 pieces, and 4 pieces were eaten.

$$\frac{10}{10} - \frac{4}{10} = \underline{\quad}$$

6. Louisa cut her lasagna into 8 pieces, and 7 pieces were eaten.

$$\frac{8}{8} - \frac{7}{8} = \underline{\quad}$$

Clumsy Couple

READ the paragraph, and WRITE the answers.

For their wedding, Paula and Bill got a lovely set of dishes, which included 12 dinner plates, 12 dessert plates, 8 bowls, 10 glasses, and 6 mugs. Both Paula and Bill are clumsy when they wash the dishes, and they tend to break a lot. So far they've broken 2 dinner plates, 3 dessert plates, 1 bowl, 2 glasses, and 3 mugs. Write the fraction of each kind of dish they have left.

1. Dinner plates ____

2. Dessert plates ____

3. Bowls ____

4. Glasses ____

5. Mugs ____

Rows of Robots

WRITE the fraction and decimal of blue robots for each row.

HINT: Three tenths can be written as both $\frac{3}{10}$ and 0.3.

1.

$$\frac{7}{10} \quad 0.7$$

2.

$$\underline{} \quad \underline{}$$

3.
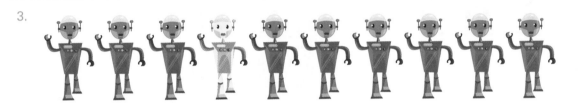

$$\underline{} \quad \underline{}$$

4.
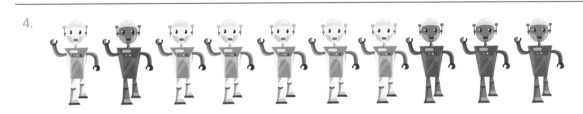

$$\underline{} \quad \underline{}$$

5.

$$\underline{} \quad \underline{}$$

6.

$$\underline{} \quad \underline{}$$

Recognizing Decimals

Piggy Bank

Decimals are used to represent dollars and cents. WRITE the value of the money on each piggy bank.

1.

$ _____

2.

$ _____

3.

$ _____

4.

$ _____

5.

$ _____

6.

$ _____

Track and Field

The times for the 50-yard dash are shown in seconds. WRITE the numbers 1 through 10 so that 1 is the fastest time and 10 is the slowest time.

	Runner	Time (in Seconds)	Rank
1.	Walter Park	7.04	_____
2.	Katie Olsen	6.23	_____
3.	Mike Green	6.08	_____
4.	Carlos Gonzales	5.94	_____
5.	Ethan Jensen	7.32	_____
6.	Nia Brown	5.82	_____
7.	Chad Guzi	6.46	_____
8.	Sarah Farmer	5.86	_____
9.	Lisa Gallagher	6.01	_____
10.	Aasif Nurang	6.59	_____

Gassing Up

CIRCLE the city in each row with the lowest average price for gasoline. Prices are shown per gallon converted to U.S. dollars.

1. San Francisco
   $3.09 per gallon

   Taipei
   $2.84 per gallon

   Milan
   $5.96 per gallon

2. Havana
   $3.03 per gallon

   Prague
   $4.19 per gallon

   Atlanta
   $2.29 per gallon

3. Copenhagen
   $5.93 per gallon

   Dublin
   $4.78 per gallon

   Lisbon
   $5.35 per gallon

4. Miami
   $2.42 per gallon

   Salt Lake City
   $2.58 per gallon

   Johannesburg
   $2.62 per gallon

5. Madrid
   $4.55 per gallon

   Tokyo
   $4.24 per gallon

   Budapest
   $4.94 per gallon

6. Caracas
   $0.12 per gallon

   Kuwait City
   $0.78 per gallon

   Cairo
   $0.65 per gallon

Plus Tax

WRITE the total cost of each item when sales tax is added.

1.

Price	$ 24.25
Tax	$ 1.52
Total	$

2.

Price	$ 17.60
Tax	$ 1.10
Total	$

3.

Price	$ 47.45
Tax	$ 2.97
Total	$

4.

Price	$ 19.99
Tax	$ 1.25
Total	$

5.

Price	$ 36.85
Tax	$ 2.30
Total	$

6.

Price	$ 62.50
Tax	$ 3.91
Total	$

Ask the Judges

The winner of the gymnastics competition is the gymnast with the highest score out of 20 possible points. ADD each gymnast's scores. Then CIRCLE the winning gymnast.

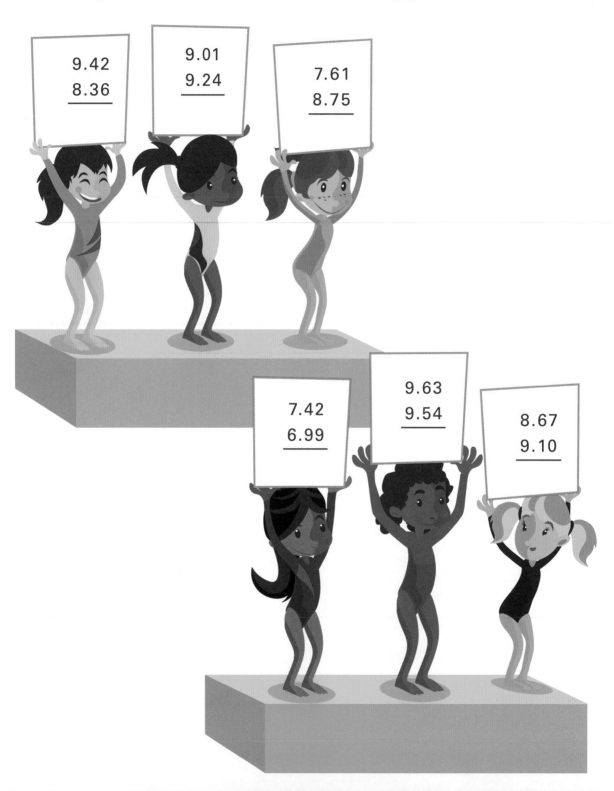

Piggy Bank

WRITE the amount that will be in each piggy bank.

1. Gretchen has saved $35.72 in her piggy bank, and she is adding $4.12.

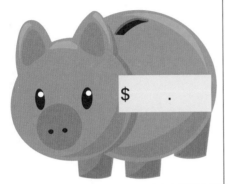

2. Hugo earned $12.90 on his paper route, which he is adding to the $48.55 already in his piggy bank.

3. Maya has $56.09 in her piggy bank, and she is adding the $10.25 she made babysitting.

4. Tommy has saved $12.94 in his piggy bank, and he is adding $5.67.

5. Elsa received $25.75 in birthday gifts and is adding it to the $72.38 in her piggy bank.

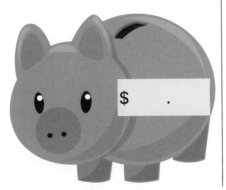

6. Ricky has $48.25 in his piggy bank, and he is adding the $1.98 he found in his pocket.

Best Price

Alex is shopping around for the best price on the new video game Night-Driver Racing. Each store has it for a different price, and Alex was able to find a coupon for each store. CIRCLE the video game with the best price if Alex uses the coupon.

$45.75

$50.99

Eddie's Electronics

$3.50 OFF

SUPERSTAR SUPERCADE

$4.75 OFF

$49.50

$52.00

Buy It Now!

$3.99 off

Gotcha Game

$7.50 off

Zoo Crew

Today the zoologists are preparing the Miniscule Creatures exhibit at the zoo. They are taking measurements in centimeters (cm) of the zoo's smallest animals to include in the exhibit. These animals are shown at actual size! WRITE each measurement as a decimal.

1. Pygmy Seahorse

_____ cm tall

2. Virgin Gorda Least Gecko

_____ cm long

3. Kitti's Hog-Nosed Bat

_____ cm long

4. Bee Hummingbird

_____ cm tall

5. Threadsnake _____ cm long

6. Speckled Padloper Tortoise

_____ cm long

Missing Measurements

All of these items have been measured, but each is missing its unit of measure. WRITE *mm*, *cm*, *m*, or *km* after each measurement.

HINT: Remember, 1 centimeter is equal to 10 millimeters (mm), 1 meter (m) is equal to 100 centimeters, and 1 kilometer (km) is equal to 1,000 meters.

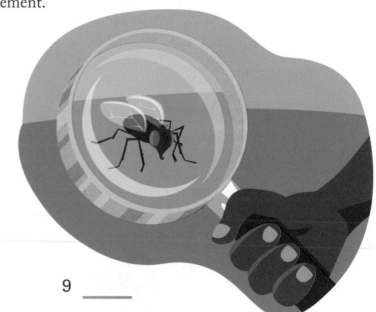

1. Length of an eyelash   9 _____

2. Distance from Boston to Philadelphia   517 _____

3. Deepest point in Lake Michigan   281 _____

4. Length of a crayon   8.9 _____

5. Size of a fly   14 _____

6. Length of an airplane   76.4 _____

7. Elevation of Mount Everest   8.49 _____

8. Size of a caterpillar   5.2 _____

9. Length of a chopstick   22.6 _____

10. Thickness of a workbook   8 _____

11. Height of a giraffe   5.3 _____

12. Length of the Golden Gate Bridge   2.74 _____

Correct Conversions

Help each person convert a measurement. WRITE the equivalent measurement.

HINT: Remember, 1 centimeter is equal to 10 millimeters (mm), 1 meter (m) is equal to 100 centimeters, and 1 kilometer (km) is equal to 1,000 meters.

1. Vanessa ran 3 kilometers.
   How many meters did she run?   _____ m

2. Benjamin drew a chalk line that is 4 meters long.
   How many centimeters long is the line?   _____ cm

3. Christina grew her fingernails to be 2 centimeters long.
   How many millimeters long are her fingernails?   _____ mm

4. Akim is 200 centimeters tall.
   How many meters tall is he?   _____ m

5. Haley found a bug that is 16 millimeters long.
   How many centimeters long is the bug?   _____ cm

6. Gabriel walked 2,500 meters.
   How many kilometers did he walk?   _____ km

7. Anna has a small red ruby that is 0.2 centimeters wide.
   How many millimeters wide is the ruby?   _____ mm

8. Andrew caught a fish that is a $\frac{1}{2}$ meter long.
   How many centimeters long is the fish?   _____ cm

Rainy Days

A rain gauge measures how much rain has fallen. WRITE the number of inches (in.) of rain that has fallen at each location. WRITE each measurement as a mixed number.

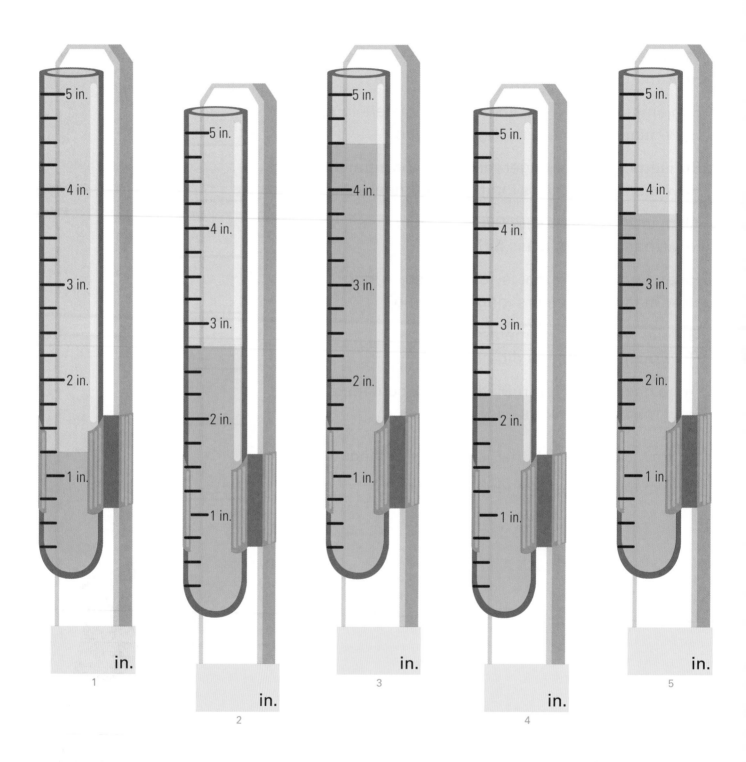

Missing Measurements

All of these items have been measured, but each is missing its unit of measure. WRITE *in.*, *ft*, *yd*, or *mi* after each measurement.

HINT: Remember, 1 foot (ft) is equal to 12 inches (in.), 1 yard (yd) is equal to 3 feet, and 1 mile (mi) is equal to 1,760 yards.

APATOSAURUS

1. Length of a football field   120 _____

2. Distance around the Earth at the equator   24,901 _____

3. Height of a person $5\frac{3}{4}$ _____

4. Length of a pen $5\frac{1}{2}$ _____

5. Length of a surfboard   9 _____

6. Size of a table   72 _____

7. Length of an apatosaurus skeleton   25 _____

8. Length of an island $10\frac{1}{2}$ _____

9. Size of a fingernail $\frac{1}{2}$ _____

10. Height of a room   12 _____

11. Distance from Vancouver to Seattle   140 _____

12. Length of an earthworm $\frac{5}{12}$ _____

Fine Fabrics

Fabric is usually sold by the yard, but these fabric measurements are listed in inches and feet. WRITE each measurement in yards. Write the answer as a fraction or a mixed number.

HINT: Remember, 1 foot (ft) is equal to 12 inches (in.), and 1 yard (yd) is equal to 3 feet.

1. Silk: 36 in. _____ yd   2. Chiffon: 6 ft _____ yd

3. Poplin: 108 in. _____ yd   4. Wool: 3 ft _____ yd

5. Cotton: 72 in. _____ yd   6. Fleece: 18 ft _____ yd

7. Rayon: 18 in. _____ yd   8. Satin: 2 ft _____ yd

9. Twill: 6 in. _____ yd   10. Denim: 1 ft _____ yd

11. Linen: 48 in. _____ yd   12. Corduroy: 14 ft _____ yd

Picket Fences

The Beckets would like to put picket fences around their pool, their swing set area, their vegetable garden, and their entire backyard. WRITE the perimeter of each part. Then WRITE the total length of fence they will need.

HINT: To find the perimeter of something, add the length of each side.

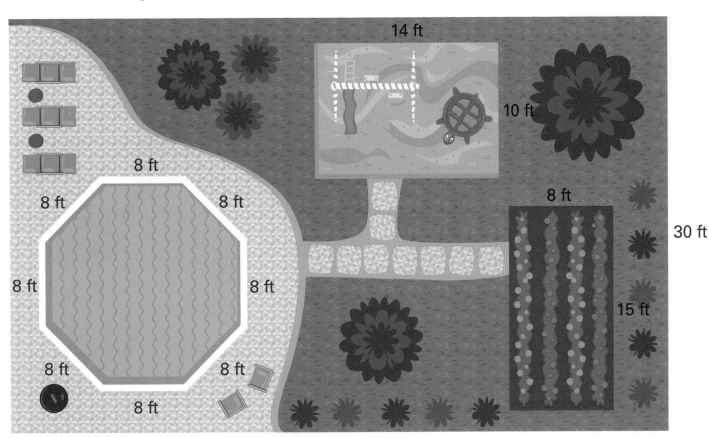

1. Pool _____ ft

2. Vegetable garden _____ ft

3. Swing set area _____ ft

4. Backyard _____ ft

5. Total length of fence _____ ft

Kite Competition

Four children have entered their kites into a kite competition. To participate in the competition, the kite must have a perimeter of 46 inches or more. WRITE the perimeter of each kite. Then CIRCLE the kite that is too small to participate.

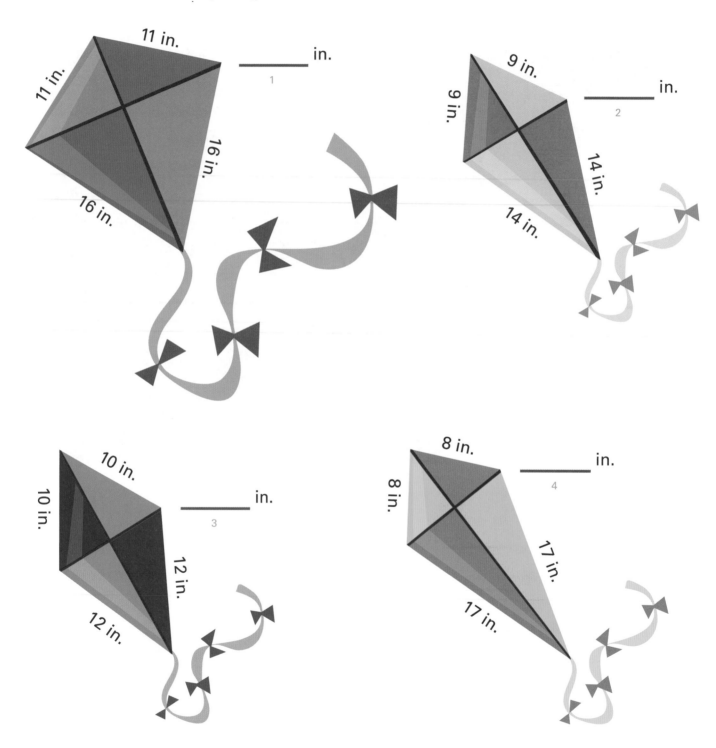

Signature Signs

Signature Signs will custom design a sign for any business. The cost of a sign is determined by the area of the sign. WRITE the area of each sign.

HINT: To find the area of a sign, multiply the length by the width.

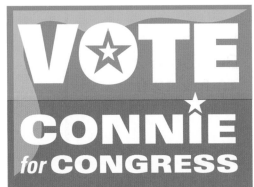

18 in.

24 in.

_____ sq in.
1

18 in.

30 in.

_____ sq in.
2

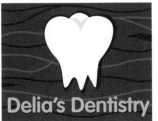

9 in.

12 in.

_____ sq in.
3

14 ft

48 ft

_____ sq ft
4

Real Estate Listing

When people are buying a home, one of the first things they look for is the number of square feet. WRITE the area of each room. Then WRITE the total number of square feet for this apartment.

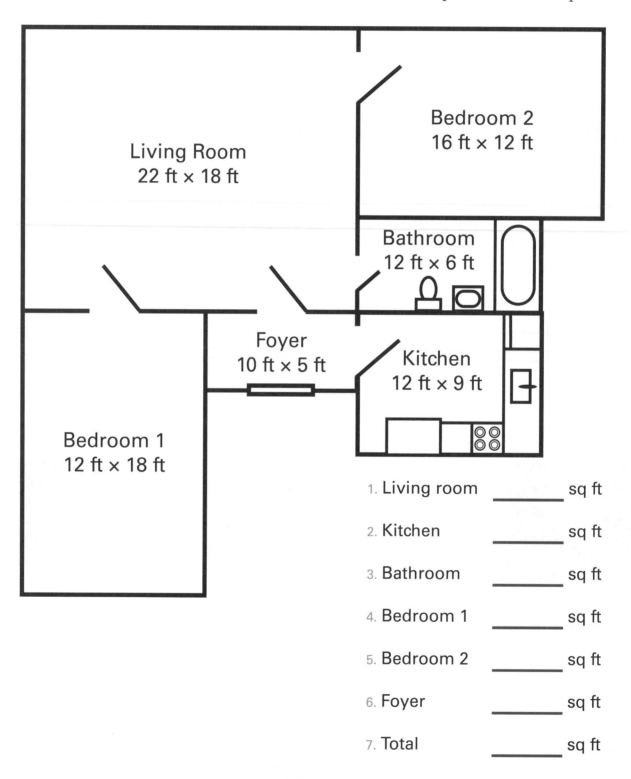

1. Living room _____ sq ft

2. Kitchen _____ sq ft

3. Bathroom _____ sq ft

4. Bedroom 1 _____ sq ft

5. Bedroom 2 _____ sq ft

6. Foyer _____ sq ft

7. Total _____ sq ft

That Can't Be Right

CIRCLE the person who is most likely stretching the truth.

HINT: Remember, 1 pound (lb) is equal to 16 ounces (oz), and 1 ton (T) is equal to 2,000 pounds.

My friends and I baked so many cookies yesterday that together we used a whole 5-pound bag of flour.

I was watching a game show this afternoon, and the grand prize for the winner was one ton of candy bars from the show's sponsor!

I got a box full of books in the mail today. It weighed 40 pounds, and I could hardly lift it.

I had a checkup yesterday, and the doctor told me I weigh 85 ounces.

Missing Measurements

All of these items have been weighed, but each is missing its unit of measure. WRITE *oz*, *lb*, or *T* after each measurement.

HINT: Remember, 1 pound (lb) is equal to 16 ounces (oz), and 1 ton (T) is equal to 2,000 pounds.

1. Elephant   10 _____

2. Tomato   8 _____

3. Full suitcase   45 _____

4. Mouse   6 _____

5. Barbell   25 _____

6. 18-wheeler truck   32 _____

7. Dictionary   96 _____

8. Baby   7 _____

9. Car   5,000 _____

10. 12-foot steel beam   1 _____

11. Laptop computer   64 _____

12. Mountain bike   25 _____

Pound Puppies

Each puppy's weight is shown in ounces. WRITE each puppy's weight in pounds.

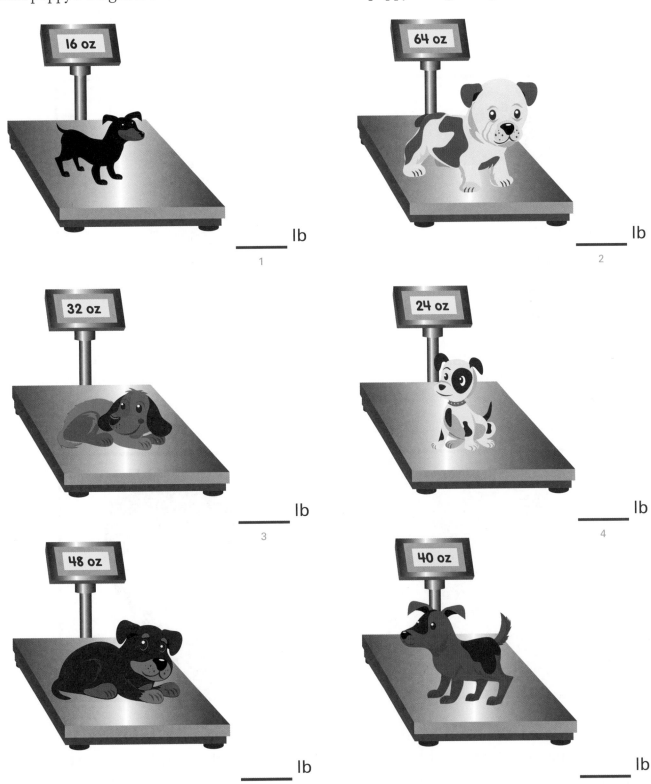

16 oz

_____ lb
1

64 oz

_____ lb
2

32 oz

_____ lb
3

24 oz

_____ lb
4

48 oz

_____ lb
5

40 oz

_____ lb
6

That Can't Be Right

CIRCLE the person who is most likely stretching the truth.

HINT: Remember, 1 gram (g) is equal to 1,000 milligrams (mg), and 1 kilogram (kg) is equal to 1,000 grams.

Today we had 150 kilograms of sand delivered to fill our backyard sandbox.

I bought a huge pumpkin at the pumpkin patch. It weighs 10,000 milligrams!

I discovered a small caterpillar on the sidewalk. It couldn't have weighed more than 4 grams.

At the museum we saw one of the largest diamonds in the world. It weighs almost 60 grams!

Missing Measurements

All of these items have been weighed, but each is missing its unit of measure. WRITE *mg*, *g*, or *kg* after each measurement.

HINT: Remember, 1 gram (g) is equal to 1,000 milligrams (mg), and 1 kilogram (kg) is equal to 1,000 grams.

1. Minimarshmallow   2 _____

2. Bulldozer   15,200 _____

3. Penny   3.1 _____

4. Feather   4,500 _____

5. Cell phone   135 _____

6. Flat-screen TV   99 _____

7. Jar of peanut butter   790 _____

8. Bag of groceries   4 _____

9. Cracker   3,000 _____

10. Kitten $\frac{1}{2}$ _____

11. Pencil   10 _____

12. Pair of sneakers   482 _____

Kate's Kitchen

Today in Kate's Kitchen, Kate is making dumplings. The weight of each ingredient is in kilograms, but Kate's recipe is in grams. WRITE the weight of each ingredient in grams.

1. 1 kg flour _____ g

2. 0.6 kg ground meat _____ g

3. 0.2 kg chopped scallions _____ g

4. 0.3 kg shredded carrots _____ g

Angled Alphabet

An **angle** is formed when two lines meet. There are three different types of angles: right, acute, and obtuse. LOOK at the angles, and ANSWER the questions.

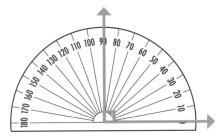

A **right** angle is an angle measuring exactly 90°, indicated by the ⌐ symbol in the corner.

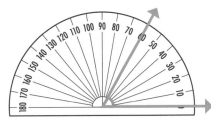

An **acute** angle is any angle measuring less than 90°.

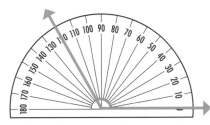

An **obtuse** angle is any angle measuring more than 90°.

1. Circle each letter that has at least one right angle.

M E C L J H

2. Circle each letter that has at least one acute angle.

A T W Z F N

3. Circle each letter that has at least one obtuse angle.

X M V Y A E

Field Trip

TAKE a walk around your neighborhood to look for angles. When you find something that forms a right, acute, or obtuse angle, WRITE it on the list.

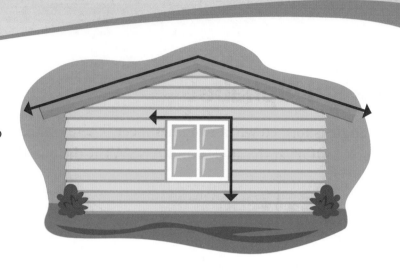

Right	
Acute	
Obtuse	

About a Shape

WRITE the name of the shape each person is thinking about.

 A **triangle** has three sides.

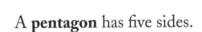 A **rectangle** has four sides.

A **square** is a special kind of rectangle that has four equal sides.

A **pentagon** has five sides.

A **hexagon** has six sides.

A **heptagon** has seven sides.

An **octagon** has eight sides.

A **nonagon** has nine sides.

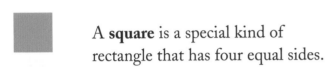
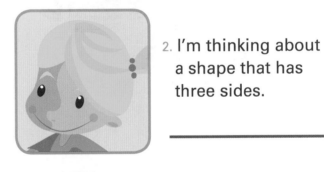

 1. I'm thinking about a shape that has eight sides.

_____

2. I'm thinking about a shape that has three sides.

_____

 3. I'm thinking about a shape that has five sides.

_____

4. I'm thinking about a shape that has four equal sides.

_____

 5. I'm thinking about a shape that has seven sides.

_____

 6. I'm thinking about a shape that has nine sides.

_____

Hockey Jerseys

Every hockey team in the league is named after a shape, and the teams like to have the shape on their jerseys. CIRCLE the back of the jersey that matches the front of the jersey.

Shape Search

THINK of things that have the shape of a pentagon, hexagon, heptagon, octagon, and nonagon. WRITE the name of each thing next to its shape.

HINT: Stuck for ideas? Ask a parent for help typing the shape name into an Internet search, and see what you can discover!

Pentagon	
Hexagon	
Heptagon	
Octagon	
Nonagon	

High Score

These four kids are all trying to get the high score in a video game where they earn points by blasting shapes. MULTIPLY each shape by the correct number of points. Then ADD their scores, and CIRCLE the person with the highest score.

Pentagon = 5 points   Heptagon = 7 points   Nonagon = 9 points
Hexagon = 6 points   Octagon = 8 points

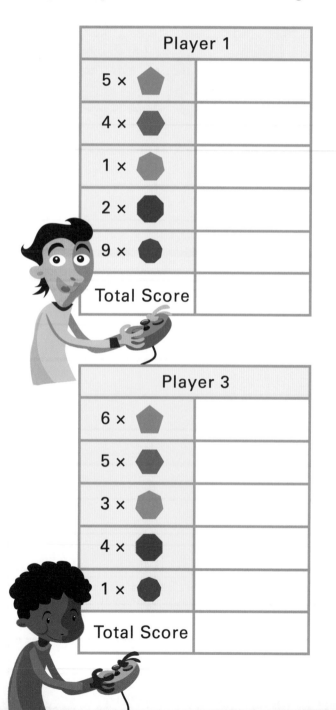

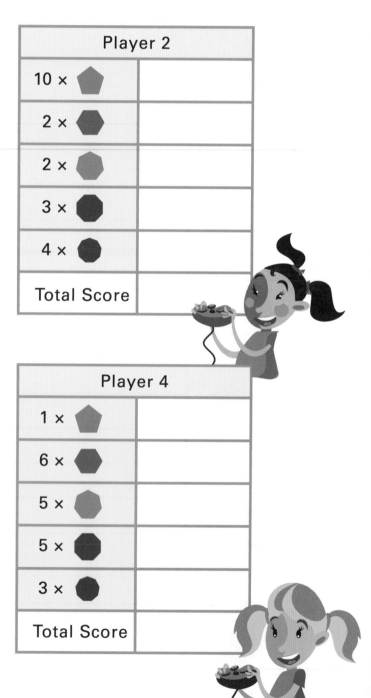

Player 1	
5 × ⬠	
4 × ⬡	
1 × ⬣	
2 × ⯃	
9 × ⬟	
Total Score	

Player 2	
10 × ⬠	
2 × ⬡	
2 × ⬣	
3 × ⯃	
4 × ⬟	
Total Score	

Player 3	
6 × ⬠	
5 × ⬡	
3 × ⬣	
4 × ⯃	
1 × ⬟	
Total Score	

Player 4	
1 × ⬠	
6 × ⬡	
5 × ⬣	
5 × ⯃	
3 × ⬟	
Total Score	

Save the Day

The Mighty Vertex has arrived at the remote island where the dastardly villain The Shape Shifter is hiding. All of the buildings are a different shape, but The Shape Shifter is hiding in a building that has seven vertices. CIRCLE the building where The Shape Shifter is hiding to help The Mighty Vertex locate him with his vertex vision.

HINT: A vertex is the point where two sides meet.

Angle Art

Each person was asked to draw a shape with a specific number of angles. CIRCLE the shapes that do not match the angles listed.

HINT: Two lines connected by a vertex form an angle.

Draw a shape that has four right angles.

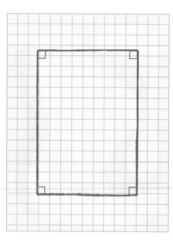

Draw a shape that has seven obtuse angles.

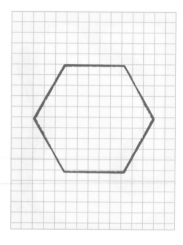

Draw a shape that has one right angle and two acute angles.

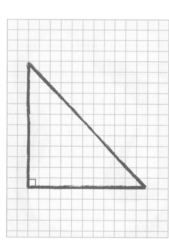

Draw a shape that has two acute angles and two obtuse angles.

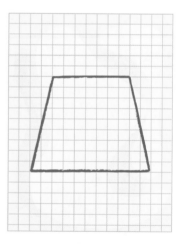

Draw a shape that has one right angle and four obtuse angles.

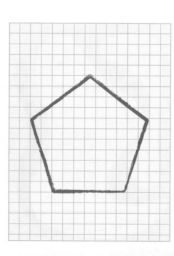

Draw a shape that has nine obtuse angles.

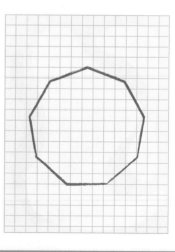

Shopper's Search

CIRCLE the package that each person is describing.

 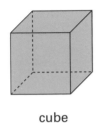 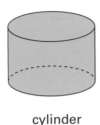  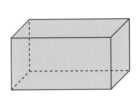 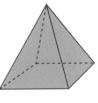

sphere · cube · cylinder · cone · rectangular prism · square pyramid

1. Can you help me? I'm looking for something for breakfast that comes in a cylinder.

2. I'm looking for a toy sphere for my son. Can you help me find something?

3. Do you have that fancy kind of candy that comes in a cube box? That's what I'd like.

Glass Towers

WRITE the number of edges and vertices on each tower.

HINT: In a three-dimensional shape, an edge is where two faces meet, and a vertex is where three or more edges meet.

1. _____ edges   2. _____ edges   3. _____ edges   4. _____ edges   5. _____ edges

_____ vertices   _____ vertices   _____ vertices   _____ vertices   _____ vertices

Save the Day

Criminal mastermind Two Square Face is on the loose and ready to steal again, unless Owlboy can stop him. He is known for stealing only precious crystals that have at least two square faces. CIRCLE the crystals at the museum exhibit that will need extra protection from Owlboy.

HINT: On a three-dimensional shape, a face is the shape formed by the edges.

About a Shape

WRITE the name of the shape each person is thinking about.

1. I'm thinking about a shape that has two faces that are circles.

_____

2. I'm thinking about a shape that has 12 edges and no square faces.

_____

3. I'm thinking about a shape that has one face that is a circle.

_____

4. I'm thinking about a shape that has edges that are all the same length.

_____

5. I'm thinking about a shape that has five vertices.

_____

6. I'm thinking about a shape that has no edges or vertices.

_____

Find the Flag

CIRCLE the flags that match each description.

HINT: Do not count the flag edges. Only use the flag pattern.

Intersecting lines are lines that cross one another.

Perpendicular lines intersect to form right angles.

Parallel lines never intersect and are always the same distance apart.

CIRCLE any flag that has at least one pair of intersecting lines in its design.

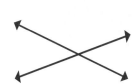
Jamaica

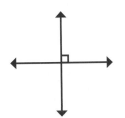
Italy

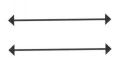
Morocco

Greece

CIRCLE any flag that has at least one pair of perpendicular lines in its design.

Denmark

Trinidad

Sweden

Jordan

CIRCLE any flag that has at least one pair of parallel lines in its design.

Bahrain

United States

Japan

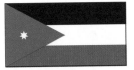
Germany

Field Trip

TAKE a walk around your neighborhood to look for intersecting, perpendicular, and parallel lines. When you find something that forms intersecting, perpendicular, or parallel lines, WRITE it on the list.

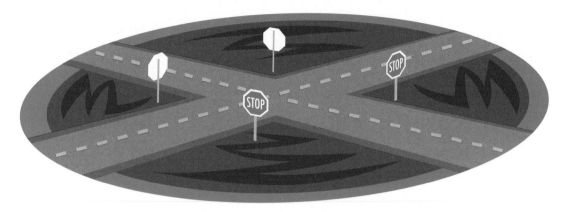

Intersecting	
Perpendicular	
Parallel	

Lots of Languages

In a survey, people were asked if they speak another language at home besides English. LOOK at the graph, and ANSWER the questions.

Languages Spoken at Home Besides English

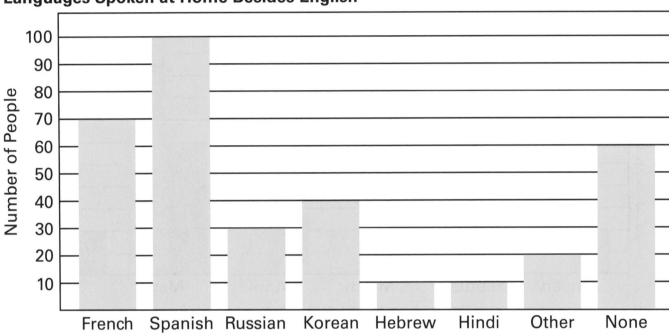

1. How many people speak Spanish at home? _____

2. How many people speak Korean at home? _____

3. How many people do not speak a language besides English at home? _____

4. How many more people speak French than Russian at home? _____

5. How many more people speak Korean than Hebrew at home? _____

6. What two languages do the same number of people speak at home?

_____

7. What are the three most popular languages other than English that people speak at home? _____

8. How many people speak a language other than English, French, Spanish, or Korean at home? _____

Bar Graphs

Entertainment News

In the past six months, two new entertainment and celebrity news Web sites, Celeb Monitor and Edith's Entertainment, have launched. This graph shows the number of visitors in thousands to each of the Web sites. LOOK at the graph, and ANSWER the questions.

Monthly Web Site Visitors

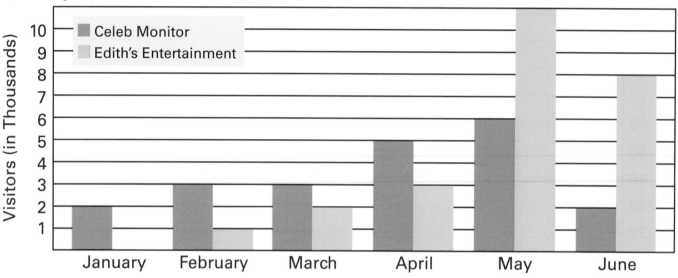

1. How many visitors did Celeb Monitor have in January?

2. In what month did Edith's Entertainment first reach 1,000 visitors?

3. In April, how many more visitors came to Celeb Monitor than Edith's Entertainment?

4. In what month did the number of visitors to Celeb Monitor stay the same as the previous month?

5. In what month did the number of visitors to both Web sites go down from the previous month?

6. One month Celeb Monitor had a Web server crash that caused the Web site to be down for a week. In what month did this likely happen?

7. One month Edith's Entertainment got an exclusive interview with a teen star that brought many new visitors. In what month did this likely happen?

Movie Tickets

A local movie theater tracked the purchase of movie tickets by kids and adults on July 1. LOOK at the graph, and ANSWER the questions.

Movie Tickets Sold on July 1

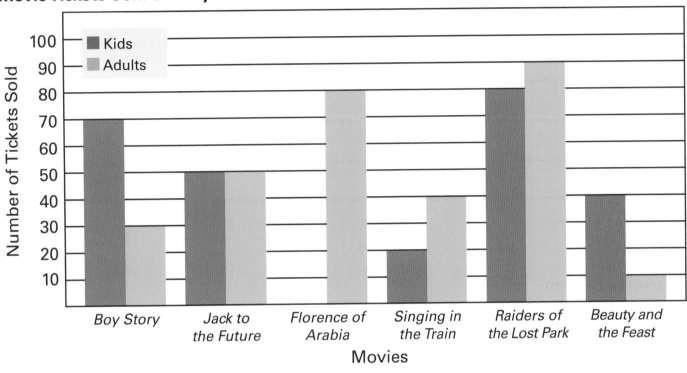

1. How many kids bought tickets to see *Boy Story* on July 1? _____

2. How many adults bought tickets to see *Florence of Arabia* on July 1? _____

3. Which movies did more kids see than adults? _____

_____

4. Which movie did the same number of kids and adults see? _____

5. Which movie is the most popular? _____

6. How likely is it that an adult will buy a ticket to see *Beauty and the Feast* on July 2?

    impossible   unlikely   likely   certain

7. How likely is it that a kid will buy a ticket to see *Florence of Arabia* on July 2?

    impossible   unlikely   likely   certain

Graph It

ASK 10 kids and 10 adults their favorite season. RECORD their answers with tally marks in the chart. Then DRAW the graph.

	Kids	Adults
Spring		
Summer		
Fall		
Winter		

Favorite Season

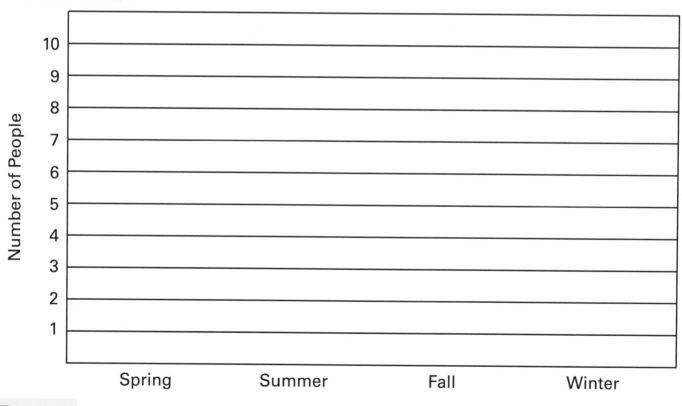

Number of People

Spring   Summer   Fall   Winter

■ Kids
■ Adults

Computer Craze

One hundred people were asked their main reason for buying a new computer. LOOK at the graph, and ANSWER the questions.

Reason for Buying a Computer

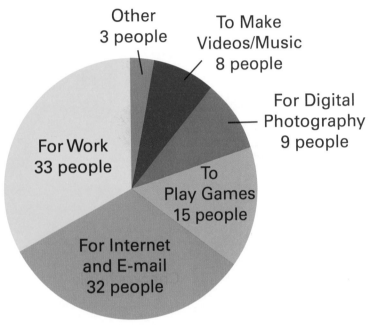

Other
3 people

To Make
Videos/Music
8 people

For Digital
Photography
9 people

For Work
33 people

To
Play Games
15 people

For Internet
and E-mail
32 people

1. How many people bought a computer for work? _____

2. How many people bought a computer to play games? _____

3. How many more people bought a computer for Internet and e-mail than for digital photography? _____

4. How many people bought a computer for videos, music or digital photography? _____

5. The number of people who bought a computer to play games can be represented as what decimal?   0.33   0.08   0.15   0.32

6. The number of people who bought a computer to make videos or music can be represented as what decimal?   0.33   0.08   0.15   0.32

7. How likely is it that someone buying a computer tomorrow will buy it for work or for Internet and e-mail?   impossible   unlikely   likely   certain

8. How likely is it that someone buying a computer tomorrow will buy it to watch movies?   impossible   unlikely   likely   certain

Favorite Flavors

Ira at Ira's Ice Cream Shop is thinking about changing ice cream flavors, so Ira graphed the ice cream flavors that people bought on a hot Saturday afternoon. LOOK at the graph, and ANSWER the questions.

Flavor Purchases on Saturday

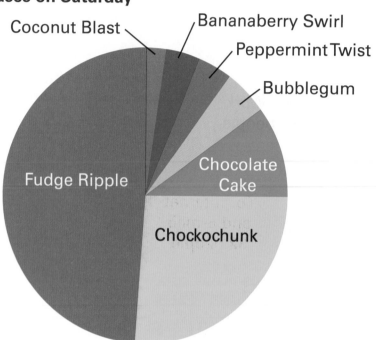

1. What is the most popular flavor? _____

2. Did more people buy Peppermint Twist or Coconut Blast? _____

3. What flavors were more popular than Chocolate Cake? _____

4. What two flavors sold in equal amounts? _____

5. On Saturday, no one bought one of the flavors. What flavor was it?

_____

6. About what fraction of people bought Fudge Ripple? $\frac{1}{4}$ $\frac{1}{3}$ $\frac{1}{2}$ $\frac{3}{4}$

7. About what fraction of people bought Chocochunk? $\frac{1}{4}$ $\frac{1}{3}$ $\frac{1}{2}$ $\frac{3}{4}$

8. Based on this graph, what flavor should Ira's Ice Cream Shop replace with a new flavor? _____

Pick a Graph

READ the paragraph, and CIRCLE the correct graph.

Max was curious about his friends' favorite sports. He asked 24 of his friends to tell him their favorite sport. Half of his friends prefer baseball. Six of his friends said basketball. Two friends like soccer the best. Three friends like football, and the last person said hockey is her favorite.

Which graph works best with the title "Favorite Sports of Max's Friends"?

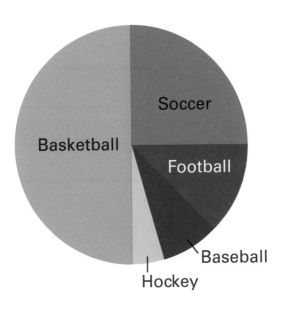

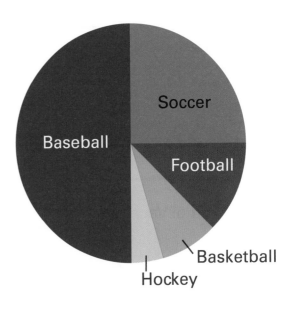

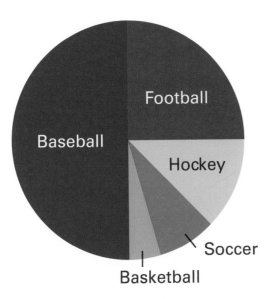

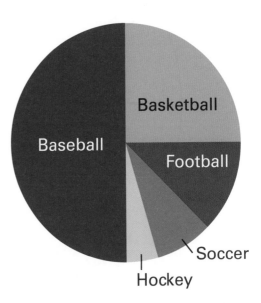

Graph It

ASK 12 people their favorite type of vacation. RECORD their answers with tally marks in the chart. Then DRAW the graph.

HINT: Figure out the fraction of each vacation type, and color that fraction in the graph. Be sure to label each color.

Favorite Vacation	Number of People
Beach	
City	
Mountains	
Amusement park	
Camping	
Other	

Favorite Type of Vacation

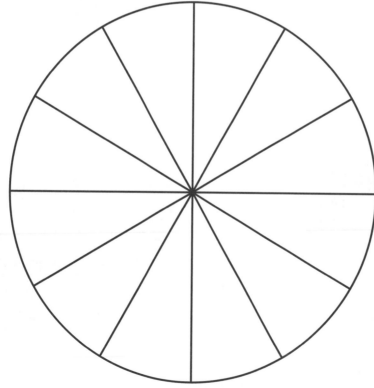

Sneaker Stock

Shecky's Shoe Store is checking its inventory of its most popular style of sneaker, which comes in eight different colors. Each X represents one pair of sneakers in stock. LOOK at the line plot, and ANSWER the questions.

Sneaker Colors in Stock

Red	Black	White	Yellow	Blue	Pink	Green	Silver
		X					
		X					
		X					
		X		X			
		X		X			
	X	X		X			
X	X	X		X			
X	X	X	X	X			
X	X	X	X	X			X
X	X	X	X	X	X		X

1. How many pairs of blue sneakers are in stock? _____

2. How many pairs of yellow sneakers are in stock? _____

3. How many more pairs of black sneakers than silver sneakers are in stock? _____

4. There is only one pair of what color sneaker left in stock? _____

5. Shecky's Shoe Store has the most pairs of what color sneaker left in stock? _____

6. What is the total number of sneaker pairs that the store has in stock? _____

7. How likely is it that someone buying a pair of the sneakers tomorrow can get them in white?   impossible   unlikely   likely   certain

8. How likely is it that someone buying a pair of the sneakers tomorrow can get them in green?   impossible   unlikely   likely   certain

Graph It

ASK 20 people about how many hours they spent watching TV in the past week. RECORD their answers by marking an X on the line plot.

Hours Spent Watching TV

```
0    1    2    3    4    5    6    7    8    9    10   11   12
```

Growing Up Fast

Starting at age two, Gracey's parents have been tracking her height each year on her birthday. LOOK at the graph, and ANSWER the questions.

Gracey's Growth Chart

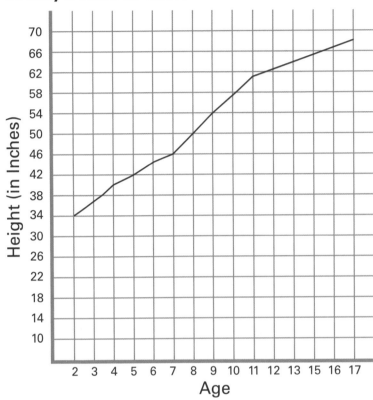

1. About how tall was Gracey at each of these ages?

   Age 2 _____ inches   Age 5 _____ inches   Age 8 _____ inches

   Age 13 _____ inches   Age 17 _____ inches

2. At what age did Gracey measure past 4 feet tall? _____

3. At what age did Gracey measure past 5 feet tall? _____

4. In what four-year period did Gracey grow 1 foot? _____ to _____

5. How likely is it that Gracey will be 84 inches tall on her 18th birthday?

   impossible   unlikely   likely   certain

Hot Sellers

This graph shows the sales of the two best-selling video games over a six-month period. LOOK at the graph, and ANSWER the questions.

Monthy Video Game Sales

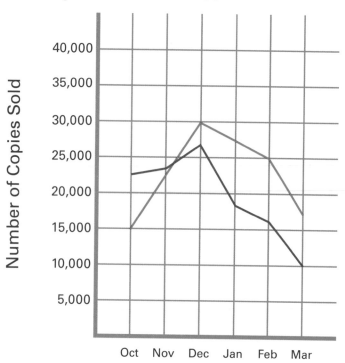

——— Roller Derby Rampage
——— Precious Pet

1. About how many copies of *Roller Derby Rampage* sold in October? _____

2. About how many copies of *Precious Pet* sold in October? _____

3. In what month did *Roller Derby Rampage* sell about 25,000 copies? _____

4. In what month did *Precious Pet* sell about 10,000 copies? _____

5. About how many total copies of *Roller Derby Rampage* sold from November to January? _____

6. About how many copies of both games combined sold in February? _____

7. What month had the highest sales for both games? _____

8. Why do you think that was? _____

Hotter or Colder?

The Johnsons live in Los Angeles, but they are thinking about moving to either Seattle or Phoenix. The weather is a factor in their decision. LOOK at the graph, and ANSWER the questions.

Average High Temperatures

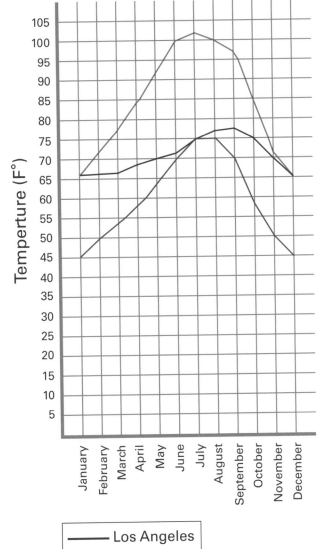

Los Angeles
Phoenix
Seattle

1. What is the average high temperature in Seattle for January? _____

2. What is the average high temperature in Seattle for June? _____

3. What is the average high temperature in Phoenix for June? _____

4. What is the average high temperature in Phoenix for October? _____

5. In what two months is it about 20 degrees hotter in Phoenix than in Los Angeles?

_____

6. In what two months is it about 15 degrees colder in Seattle than in Los Angeles?

_____

7. If the Johnsons want summers with a similar high temperature to Los Angeles, where should they move?

_____

8. If the Johnsons want winters with a similar high temperature to Los Angeles, where should they move?

_____

Graph It

Challenge a friend to a friendly reading competition to see who can read more pages in a week. RECORD the number of pages each person reads each day. Then DRAW the graph.

	Name:	Name:
Day 1		
Day 2		
Day 3		
Day 4		
Day 5		
Day 6		
Day 7		

Reading Challenge

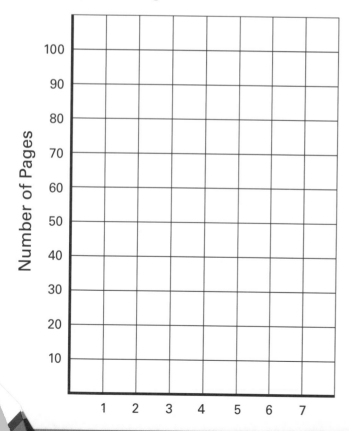

Name: _____

Name: _____

Page 213
1. 4,965
2. 10,515
3. 9,173
4. 21,340
5. 124,603
6. 76,942
7. 1,802,199

Page 214
1. Three thousand, two hundred ninety-seven
2. Forty-eight thousand, one hundred fifty-eight
3. One hundred five thousand, three hundred sixty-six
4. Five million, six hundred twelve thousand, eight hundred forty-one

Page 215

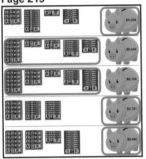

Page 216
1. 4
2. 7
3. 5
4. 1
5. 10
6. 3
7. 8
8. 2
9. 6
10. 9

Page 217
1. Benxi
2. Denver
3. Seville
4. Daqing
5. Minsk
6. New York

Page 218
1. 7
2. 2
3. 5
4. 3
5. 10
6. 1
7. 6
8. 4
9. 8
10. 9

Page 219
1. 40,000
2. 30,000
3. 60,000
4. 50,000

Page 220
1. 300,000
2. 900,000
3. 100,000
4. 800,000
5. 500,000
6. 700,000
7. 1,000,000
8. 800,000

Page 221
1. 48
2. 700
3. 50,000
4. 1,400
5. 190

Page 222
Check:
1. 73
2. 1,860
3. 6,500
4. 10,000,000
5. 5

Page 223

	Candidate 1	Candidate 2	Candidate 3	Candidate 4	Candidate 5
Morning votes	44,117	30,051	53,412	34,160	27,321
Afternoon votes	23,710	42,042	21,473	35,113	41,220
Total votes	67,827	72,093	74,885	69,273	68,541

Page 224
1. 14,983
2. 42,488
3. 25,746
4. 97,629

Page 225
1. 43,036
2. 47,450
3. 43,217
4. 65,007
5. 49,714
6. 68,373

Page 226

Page 227

Page 228
1. 13,051
2. 8,503
3. 11,655
4. 4,526
5. 20,319

Page 229
1. 4,894
2. 26,553
3. 13,948
4. 24,242
5. 405
6. 44,123
7. 1,190
8. 57,083

Page 230

Page 231
1. 90,000
2. 40,000
3. 60,000
4. 50,000
5. 80,000
6. 40,000

Page 232

61,265 + 10,942 → 72207
60,000 + 10,000 = 70,000

64,427 − 33,158 → 21725
60,000 − 30,000 = 30,000

26,723 + 24,304 → 42027
30,000 + 20,000 = 50,000

88,595 − 16,913 → 71682
90,000 − 20,000 = 70,000

48,126 + 39,591 → 87717
50,000 + 40,000 = 90,000

72,088 − 63,213 → 18875
70,000 − 60,000 = 10,000

Page 233

Player 1	
4 × ●	24
5 × ●	35
9 × ●	72
0 × ●	0
2 × ●	20
Total Score	151

Player 2	
10 × ●	60
2 × ●	14
3 × ●	24
7 × ●	63
4 × ●	40
Total Score	201

Player 3	
5 × ●	30
9 × ●	63
8 × ●	64
8 × ●	72
0 × ●	0
Total Score	229

Player 4	
3 × ●	18
10 × ●	70
1 × ●	8
2 × ●	18
3 × ●	30
Total Score	144

Page 234
1. 45
2. 48
3. 25
4. 20
5. 32
6. 30
7. 36
8. 28
9. 35
10. 72
11. 20
12. 16
13. 50
14. 24
15. 45
16. 24

Page 235
1. 140
2. 75
3. 180
4. 315
5. 80
6. 360
7. 200
8. 275
9. 360
10. 195
11. 490
12. 675

Page 236
1. 360, 450
2. 300, 375
3. 128, 160
4. 352, 440
5. 256, 320
6. 204, 255
7. 328, 410
8. 308, 385

Page 237
1. 1,575
2. 1,080
3. 440
4. 1,260
5. 432
6. 1,840

Page 238
1. 3,280
2. 1,480
3. 976
4. 7,992
5. 3,072
6. 2,712
7. 5,928
8. 1,960

Page 239

Player 1	
6 × ●	36
5 × ●	35
2 × ●	16
10 × ●	90
1 × ●	10
Total Score	187

Player 2	
9 × ●	54
3 × ●	21
7 × ●	56
2 × ●	18
10 × ●	100
Total Score	249

Player 3	
7 × ●	42
4 × ●	28
6 × ●	48
3 × ●	27
2 × ●	20
Total Score	165

Player 4	
4 × ●	24
9 × ●	63
8 × ●	64
1 × ●	9
5 × ●	50
Total Score	210

Page 240
1. 9
2. 7
3. 5
4. 8
5. 6
6. 9
7. 5
8. 7
9. 4

Page 241
1. 15
2. 12
3. 19
4. 28
5. 22
6. 16

Page 242
1. 24
2. 17
3. 31
4. 22
5. 32
6. 25

Page 243
1. 35
2. 16
3. 31

Page 244
1. 6
2. 4
3. 13
4. 9
5. 12
6. 10
7. 8
8. 15

Page 245
1. $\frac{3}{8}$
2. $\frac{5}{6}$
3. $\frac{1}{7}$
4. $\frac{2}{9}$
5. $\frac{3}{4}$
6. $\frac{5}{12}$

Page 246
1. $\frac{7}{12}$
2. $\frac{3}{12}$
3. $\frac{8}{12}$
4. $\frac{4}{12}$
5. $\frac{1}{12}$
6. $\frac{4}{12}$

Answers

Page 247

Page 248

Kate's Apple Muffins
- 5/6 cup flour
- 1/3 cup sugar
- 1/4 cup brown sugar
- teaspoon cinnamon
- cup butter
- 3/4 cup chopped apples
- 1 egg

Yummy Apple Muffins
- cup flour
- 1/3 cup sugar
- cup brown sugar
- 1/3 teaspoon cinnamon
- cup butter
- cup chopped apples
- 2 eggs

Mom's Apple Muffins
- cup flour
- 1/2 cup sugar
- 1/3 cup brown sugar
- teaspoon cinnamon
- cup butter
- 3/8 cup chopped apples
- 1 egg

Page 249

1. $\frac{3}{4}$ 2. $\frac{4}{5}$

3. $\frac{6}{8}$ 4. $\frac{2}{6}$

5. $\frac{9}{10}$ 6. $\frac{4}{7}$

7. $\frac{7}{9}$ 8. $\frac{8}{8}$

Page 250

Double-Chocolate Cookies (Doubled)
- $\frac{6}{4}$ cup flour
- $\frac{2}{3}$ cup cocoa
- $\frac{2}{2}$ cup sugar
- $\frac{2}{4}$ teaspoon baking soda
- $\frac{2}{8}$ teaspoon salt
- $\frac{4}{3}$ cup chocolate chips
- $\frac{14}{8}$ cup butter

Page 251

1. $\frac{2}{6}$ 2. $\frac{3}{4}$

3. $\frac{5}{12}$ 4. $\frac{4}{9}$

5. $\frac{6}{10}$ 6. $\frac{1}{8}$

Page 252

1. $\frac{10}{12}$ 2. $\frac{9}{12}$

3. $\frac{7}{8}$ 4. $\frac{8}{10}$

5. $\frac{3}{6}$

Page 253

1. $\frac{7}{10}$ 2. $\frac{5}{10}$

3. $\frac{9}{10}$ 4. $\frac{4}{10}$

5. $\frac{2}{10}$ 6. $\frac{8}{10}$

Page 254

1. 2.48   2. 8.15
3. 11.76   4. 4.89
5. 16.05   6. 0.92

Page 255

1. 9   2. 6   3. 5
4. 3   5. 10   6. 1
7. 7   8. 2   9. 4
10. 8

Page 256

1. Taipei   2. Atlanta
3. Dublin   4. Miami
5. Tokyo   6. Caracas

Page 257

1. 25.77   2. 18.70
3. 50.42   4. 21.24
5. 39.15   6. 66.41

Page 258

9.42 / 8.36 / 17.78

9.01 / 9.24 / 18.25

7.61 / 8.75 / 16.36

7.42 / 6.99 / 14.41

9.63 / 9.54 / 19.17

8.67 / 9.10 / 17.77

Page 259

1. 39.84   2. 61.45
3. 66.34   4. 18.61
5. 98.13   6. 50.23

Page 260

$45.75
$50.99
Eddie's Electronics $3.50 OFF
SUPERSTAR SUPERGAME $4.75 OFF
$49.50
$52.00
Buy It Now! $3.99 off
Gotcha Game $7.50 off

Page 261

1. 1.6   2. 2.4   3. 3.1
4. 4.9   5. 9.7   6. 8.3

Page 262

1. mm   2. km   3. m
4. cm   5. mm   6. m
7. km   8. cm   9. cm
10. mm   11. m   12. km

Page 263

1. 3,000   2. 400   3. 20
4. 2   5. 1.6   6. 2.5
7. 2   8. 50

Page 264

1. $1\frac{1}{4}$ 2. $2\frac{3}{4}$ 3. $4\frac{1}{2}$

4. $2\frac{1}{4}$ 5. $3\frac{3}{4}$

Page 265

1. yd   2. mi   3. ft
4. in.   5. ft   6. in.
7. yd   8. mi   9. in.
10. ft   11. mi   12. ft

Page 266

1. 1   2. 2   3. 3
4. 1   5. 2   6. 6
7. $\frac{1}{2}$ 8. $\frac{2}{3}$ 9. $\frac{1}{6}$
10. $\frac{1}{3}$ 11. $1\frac{1}{3}$ 12. $4\frac{2}{3}$

Page 267

1. 64   2. 46   3. 48
4. 160   5. 318

Page 268

1. 54   2. 46
3. 44   4. 50

Page 269

1. 432   2. 540
3. 108   4. 672

Page 270

1. 396   2. 108   3. 72
4. 216   5. 192   6. 50
7. 1,034

Page 271

Page 272

1. T   2. oz   3. lb
4. oz   5. lb   6. T
7. oz   8. lb   9. lb
10. T   11. oz   12. lb

Page 273

1. 1   2. 4   3. 2
4. 1   5. 3   6. 2

Page 274

Page 275

1. mg   2. kg   3. g
4. mg   5. g   6. kg
7. g   8. kg   9. mg
10. kg   11. g   12. g

Page 276

1. 1,000   2. 600
3. 200   4. 300

Page 277

1. E, L, H
2. A, W, Z, N
3. X, Y, A

Page 278

Have someone check your answers.

Page 279

1. octagon   2. triangle
3. pentagon   4. square
5. heptagon   6. nonagon

Page 280

Page 281

Have someone check your answers.

Page 282

Player 1			Player 2	
5 × ⬟	25		10 × ⬟	50
4 × ⬢	24		2 × ⬣	12
1 × ⬢	7		2 × ⬣	14
2 × ⬢	16		3 × ⬢	24
9 × ●	81		4 × ●	36
Total Score	153		Total Score	136

Player 3			Player 4	
6 × ⬟	30		1 × ⬟	5
5 × ⬢	30		6 × ⬢	36
3 × ⬢	21		5 × ⬢	35
4 × ●	32		5 × ⬢	40
1 × ⬢	9		3 × ●	27
Total Score	122		Total Score	143

Page 283

Page 284

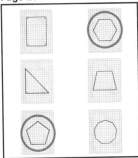

Page 285

Page 286
1. 12, 8
2. 16, 9
3. 12, 8
4. 8, 5
5. 24, 16

Page 287

Page 288
1. cylinder
2. rectangular prism
3. cone
4. cube
5. square pyramid
6. sphere

Page 289

Page 290
Have someone check
your answers.

Page 291
1. 100
2. 40
3. 60
4. 40
5. 30
6. Hebrew, Hindi
7. Spanish, French, Korean
8. 70

Page 292
1. 2,000   2. February
3. 2,000   4. March
5. June   6. June
7. May

Page 293
1. 70
2. 80
3. *Boy Story, Beauty and the Feast*
4. *Jack to the Future*
5. *Raiders of the Lost Park*
6. unlikely
7. unlikely

Page 294
Have someone check
your answers.

Page 295
1. 33   2. 15
3. 23   4. 17
5. 0.15 6. 0.08
7. likely 8. unlikely

Page 296
1. Fudge Ripple
2. Peppermint Twist
3. Chockochunk, Fudge Ripple
4. Bananaberry Swirl,
   Peppermint Twist
5. Peanut Butter Raisin
6. $\frac{1}{2}$
7. $\frac{1}{4}$
8. Peanut Butter Raisin

Page 297

Page 298
Have someone check
your answers.

Page 299
1. 7   2. 3   3. 3
4. pink   5. white 6. 32
7. likely 8. impossible

Page 300
Have someone check
your answers.

Page 301
1. 34, 42, 50, 64, 68
2. age 8
3. age 11
4. 5, 9
5. impossible

Page 302
1. 15,000
2. 22,500
3. Feburary
4. March
5. 80,000
6. 41,000
7. December
8. Games were probably
   purchased as holiday gifts.

Page 303
1. 45°F
2. 70°F
3. 100°F
4. 85°F
5. May, September
6. February, October
7. Seattle
8. Phoenix

Page 304
Have someone check
your answers.